THE CREATURE SPRANG TO ITS FEET

A LITTLE MAID

OF

PROVINCETOWN

BY

ALICE TURNER CURTIS

AUTHOR OF

A LITTLE MAID OF OLD NEW YORK
A LITTLE MAID OF OLD PHILADELPHIA
A LITTLE MAID OF MASSACHUSETTS COLONY
A LITTLE MAID OF OLD CONNECTICUT
A LITTLE MAID OF TICONDEROGA
A LITTLE MAID OF MARYLAND

ILLUSTRATED BY WUANITA SMITH

APPLEWOOD BOOKS
BEDFORD, MASSACHUSETTS

A Little Maid of Provincetown was first published by the Penn Publishing Company in 1913.

ISBN 978-1-55709-331-8

Thank you for purchasing an Applewood Book.
Applewood reprints America's lively classics—
books from the past that are still of interest to modern readers.
For a free copy of our current catalog, write to:
Applewood Books, P.O. Box 365, Bedford, MA 01730.

Library of Congress Cataloging-in-Publication Data
Curtis, Alice Turner.
    A little maid of Provincetown / by Alice Turner Curtis; illustrated by Wuanita Smith.
        p.   cm.
    Summary: During the Revolutionary War, eight-year-old Anne Nelson, living in Provincetown on Cape Cod, determines to help the patriots' cause by carrying an important message from Boston to Newburyport.
    ISBN 978-1-55709-331-8
    1. United States—History—Revolution, 1775–1783—Juvenile fiction.   [1. Massachusetts—History—Revolution, 1775–1783—Fiction.   2. United States—History—Revolution, 1775–1783—Fiction.]
I. Smith, Wuanita, ill.   II. Title
PZ7.C941Lmp   1997
[Fic]—dc21   97-3987
                                                     CIP
                                                      AC

Contents

Illustrations

A Little Maid of Provincetown

CHAPTER I

ANNE NELSON

"I DON'T know what I can do with you, I'm sure!" declared Mistress Stoddard, looking down at the small girl who stood on her door-step gazing wistfully up at her.

"A man at the wharf said that you didn't have any little girls," responded the child, "and so I thought—"

" 'Twas Joe Starkweather told you, I'll be bound," said Mrs. Stoddard. "Well, he's seven of his own to fend for."

"Seven little girls?" said Anne Nelson, in an almost terror-stricken voice, her dark eyes looking earnestly into the stern face that frowned down upon her. "And what would become of them if their mother should die, and their father be lost at sea?"

"Sure enough. You have sense, child. But the Starkweathers are all boys. Well, come in. You can take your bundle to the loft and leave it, and we'll see what I can find for you to do. How old are you?"

"Eight last March," responded Anne.

"Well, a child of eight isn't much use in a house, but maybe you can save me steps."

"Yes, indeed, Mistress Stoddard; I did a deal to help my father about the house. He said I could do as much as a woman. I can sweep out for you, and lay the table and wash the dishes, and bring in the wood and water, and—" there came a break in the little girl's voice, and the woman reached out a kindly hand and took the child's bundle.

"Come in," she said, and Anne instantly felt the tenderness of her voice. "We are poor enough, but you'll be welcome to food and shelter, child, till such time as some of your own kinsfolk send for thee."

"I have no kinsfolk," declared Anne; "my father told me that."

"Come you in; you'll have a bed and a crust while I have them to give you," declared the woman, and Anne Nelson went across the threshold and up to the bare loft, where she put her bundle down on a wooden stool and looked about the room.

There was but a narrow bed in the corner, covered with a patchwork quilt, and the wooden stool where Anne had put her bundle. The one narrow window looked off across the sandy cart tracks which served as a road toward the blue waters of Cape Cod Bay. It was early June, and the strong breath of the sea filled the rough little house, bringing with it the fragrance of the wild cherry blossoms and an odor of pine from the scrubby growths on the low line of hills back of the little settlement.

It was just a year ago, Anne remembered, as she unwrapped her bundle, that she and her father had sailed across the harbor from Ipswich, where her mother had died.

"We will live here, at the very end of the world, where a man may think as he pleases," her father had said, and had moved their few household possessions into a three-roomed house near the shore. Then he had given his time to fishing, leaving Anne alone in the little house to do as she pleased.

She was a quiet child, and found entertainment in building sand houses on the beach, in wandering along the shore searching for bright shells and smooth pebbles, and in doing such simple household tasks as her youth admitted. A week before her appearance at Mrs. Stoddard's door, John Nelson had gone out in his fishing-boat, and now he had been given up as lost. No sign of him had been seen by the other fishermen, and it was generally believed by his neighbors that his sloop had foundered and that John Nelson had perished.

Some there were, however, who declared John Nelson to be a British spy, and hesitated not to say that he had sailed away to join some vessel of the British fleet with information as to the convenience of the harbor of Provincetown, and with such other news as he had brought from Ipswich and the settlements nearer Boston. For it was just before the war of the American Revolution, when men were watched sharply and taken to task speedily for any lack of loyalty to the American colonies. And John Nelson had many a time declared that he believed England meant well by her American possessions,— a statement which set many of his neighbors against him.

"'Mean well,' indeed!" Joseph Starkweather had replied to his neighbor's remark. "When they have closed the port of Boston, so that no ship but the king's war-ships dare go in and out? Even our fishing-boats are closely watched. Already the Boston people are beginning to need many things. Americans are not going to submit to feeding British soldiers while their own men go hungry."

But now Joseph Starkweather was the only man who interested himself in the lonely child. Day after day of that first week of her father's absence Anne had stayed close to the little house, looking hopefully out across the harbor for a sight of his boat; and day after day Joseph Starkweather had come lounging down the beach to speak with the child, to ask her what she had for breakfast, and if she slept safe and unafraid.

"The meal is gone," she told him one morning, "and I do not sleep now—I wait and listen for my father;" and then it was that he told her she must seek another home.

"You are too young to stay alone," he said; "pick up a bundle of your clothes and go to Mrs. Stoddard on the hill. She hasn't a chick or child of her own. Like as not you'll be a blessing to her." And Anne, used to obedience and sorrow, obeyed.

There was nothing of much value in the small house, but on the day after Anne's entrance as a member of the Stoddard family, Captain Stoddard loaded the poor sticks of furniture on a handcart, and pulled it through the sandy tracks to his cottage door.

"It's the child of an English spy you're giving shelter to," he had said, when Martha Stoddard had told him that Anne was to live with them, "and she'll bring no luck to the house." But his wife had made no response; the dark-eyed, elfish-looking child had already found a place in the woman's heart.

"I don't eat so very much," Anne announced as Mrs. Stoddard gave her a bowl of corn mush and milk when she came down-stairs.

"You'll eat what you want in this house, child," answered her new friend, and Anne ate hungrily.

"Now come to the door, Anne, and I'll brush out this tangle of hair of yours," said Mrs. Stoddard; "and after this you must keep it brushed and braided neatly. And bring down your other frock. I'll be doing some washing this afternoon, and I venture to say your frock is in need of it."

The first few days in the Stoddard family seemed almost unreal to Anne. She no longer watched for her father's boat, she no longer wandered about the beach, playing in the sand and hunting for shells. Her dresses were not now the soiled and ragged covering which had served as frocks, but stout cotton gowns, made from a skirt of Mrs. Stoddard's, and covered with a serviceable apron. A sunbonnet of striped cotton covered the dark head, and Anne was as neat and well-dressed as the other children of the settlement. To be sure her slender feet were bare and tanned, and hardened by exposure; but there was not a child in the neighborhood who wore shoes until the frost came, and Mrs. Stoddard was already making plans for Anne's winter footgear.

"I'll trade off something for some moccasins for the child before fall," she had resolved; "some of the Chatham Indians will get down this way when the beach plums begin to ripen, and will be glad of molasses, if I am lucky enough to have it."

For those were the days when the little coast settlements had but few luxuries, and on Cape Cod the settlers were in fear of the British. Provincetown was especially exposed, and at that time there were but thirty houses; and the people had no established communication with the outside world. The sea was their thoroughfare, as a journey over the sandy country from Provincetown to Boston was almost impossible. News was a long time in reaching the little settlement of fishermen. But they knew that King George III had resolved to punish Boston for destroying his cargoes of tea, and had made Salem the seat of government in the place of Boston. Warships from England hovered about the coast, and the children of Provincetown were quick to recognize these unwelcome craft.

"Mistress Stoddard," said Anne one morning, when she had returned from driving the cow to the enclosed pasturage at some little distance from the house, "Jimmie Starkweather says there is a big ship off Race Point, and that it is coming into harbor here. He says 'tis a British ship, and that like as not the men will land and burn down the houses and kill all the cows." Anne looked at Mrs. Stoddard questioningly.

"Nonsense!" responded the good woman. "Jimmie was but trying to make you afraid. 'Twas he sent thee running home last week in fear of a wolf that he told you was prowling about."

"But there is a ship, Mistress Stoddard. I went up the hill and looked, and 'tis coming along like a great white bird."

"Like enough. The big ships go up toward Boston and Salem on every fair day. You know that well, child."

"This seems a different kind," persisted Anne; and at last Mrs. Stoddard's curiosity was aroused, and with Anne close beside her she walked briskly up to the hill and looked anxiously across the blue waters.

" 'Tis much nearer, now," said Anne. "See, it's coming to—'twill anchor."

"Sure enough," answered Mrs. Stoddard. "Jimmie Starkweather is a wise lad. 'Tis a British man-of-war. Trouble is near at hand, child."

"Will they kill our cow?" questioned Anne. "Jimmie said they would, and eat her," and Anne's voice trembled; for the small brown cow was the nearest approach to a pet that the little girl had. It seemed a loss hardly to be borne if "Brownie" was to be sacrificed.

"It's like enough they will," replied Mrs. Stoddard. "They'll be sending their boats ashore and taking what they can see. Run back to the pasture, Anne, and drive Brownie down the further slope toward the salt-meadow. There's good feed for her beyond the

wood there, and she'll not wander far before nightfall, and she will not be quickly seen there."

Anne needed no urging. With another look toward
the big ship, she fled back along the sandy road
toward the pasture, and in a short time the brown
cow, much surprised and offended, was being driven
at a run down the pasture slope, around the grove of
scrubby maples to the little valley beyond.

Anne waited until Brownie had sufficiently recov-
ered from her surprise to begin feeding again, apparently well content with her new pasturage, and then
walked slowly back toward the harbor. The village
seemed almost deserted. The children were not playing about the boats; there was no one bringing water
from the spring near the shore, and as Anne looked
out toward the harbor, she saw two more big ships
coming swiftly toward anchorage.

"Poor Brownie!" she said aloud, for if there was
danger in one ship she was sure that three meant that
there was no hope for the gentle brown cow which
she had just driven to a place of safety.

Before night a boatload of British sailors had landed, filled their water barrels at the spring, bought
some young calves of Joseph Starkweather and
returned quietly to their ships.

"They seem civil enough," said Captain Stoddard
that night as he talked the newcomers over with his

wife. "They know we could make no stand against them, but they treated Joseph Starkweather fairly enough."

Anne listened eagerly. "Will they take Brownie?" she asked.

"Indeed they won't if I can help it," answered Mrs. Stoddard; "we'll not drive the creature back and forth while the British are about. I can slip over the hill with a bucket and milk her night and morning. She's gentle, and there's no need of letting the pirates see how sleek and fat the creature is."

"And may I go with you, Mistress Stoddard?" asked Anne.

"Of course, child," answered Mrs. Stoddard, smilingly.

After Anne had gone up to the loft to bed Captain Stoddard said slowly: "She seems a good child."

"That she does, Enos. Good and careful of her clothes, and eager to be of help to me. She saves me many a step."

" 'Tis John Nelson, they say, who has brought the Britishers into harbor," responded Captain Enos slowly. "Joseph Starkweather swears that one of the sailors told him so when he bargained for the calves."

"Anne's not to blame!" declared Mrs. Stoddard loyally, but there was a note of anxiety in her voice; "as you said yourself, Enos, she's a good child."

"I'll not be keeping her if it proves true," declared the man stubbornly. "True it is that they ask no military duty of any man in Provincetown, but we're loyal folk just the same. We may have to barter with the British to save our poor lives, instead of turning guns on them as we should; but no man shall say that I took in a British spy's child and cared for it."

"They'd but say you did a Christian deed at the most," said his wife. "You're not a hard man, Enos."

"I'll not harbor a traitor's child," he insisted, and Mrs. Stoddard went sorrowfully to bed and lay sleepless through the long night, trying to think of some plan to keep Anne Nelson safe and well cared for until peaceful days should come again.

And Anne, too, lay long awake, wondering what she could do to protect the little brown cow which now rested so securely on the further side of the hill.

CHAPTER II

ANNE WINS A FRIEND

"Come, Anne," called Mrs. Stoddard at so early an hour the next morning that the June sun was just showing itself above the eastern horizon.

"Yes, Mistress Stoddard," answered the little girl promptly, and in a few minutes she came down the steep stairs from the loft.

"It is early to call you, child," said the good woman kindly, "but the captain has made an early start for the fishing grounds, and I liked not to leave you alone in the house in these troublous times; and so eat your porridge and we'll go and milk Brownie."

Anne hastened to obey; and in a few moments the two were making their way up the slope through the fragrant bayberry bushes, and breathing in the sweet morning air. No one else seemed astir in the little settlement. Now and then a flutter of some wild bird would betray that they had stepped near some low-nesting bird; and the air was full of the morning songs and chirrupings of robins, red-winged blackbirds, song sparrows, and of many sea-loving birds which built their nests among the sand-hills, but found their food upon the shore.

Anne noticed all these things as they walked along, but her thoughts were chiefly occupied with other things. There was one question she longed to ask Mrs. Stoddard, yet almost feared to ask. As they reached the summit of the hill and turned for a look at the beautiful harbor she gained courage and spoke:

"Mistress Stoddard, will you please to tell me what a 'spy' is?"

"A spy? and why do you wish to know, Anne?" responded her friend; "who has been talking to you of spies?"

"Is it an ill-seeming word?" questioned the child anxiously. "The Cary children did call it after me yesterday when I went to the spring."

"Did they that!" exclaimed Mrs. Stoddard angrily, "and what reply did you make, Anne?"

The little girl shook her head. "I said nothing. I knew not what they might mean. Does it mean an orphan child, Mistress Stoddard?" and the little girl lifted her dark eyes appealingly.

"I will tell you its meaning, Anne, and then you will see that it has naught to do with little girls. A 'spy' is like this: Suppose some one should wish to know if I kept my house in order, and what I gave the captain for dinner, and could not find out, and so she came to you and said, 'Anne Nelson, if you will tell me about the Stoddard household, and open the door that I may come in and see for myself, I will give thee a shilling and a packet of sweets'; then, if you should agree to the bargain, then you could be called a spy."

"But I would not do such a thing!" declared Anne, a little flash of resentment in her dark eyes. "Do the Cary children think me like that? I will throw water on them when next we meet at the spring—aye, and sand."

"Nay, Anne," reproved Mrs. Stoddard, but she was not ill-pleased at the child's spirit. "Then you would be as bad as they. It does not matter what they may say: that is neither here nor there. If you be an honest-thinking child and do well they cannot work harm against you."

As they talked they had walked on and now heard a low "Moo!" from behind a bunch of wild cherry trees.

"There's Brownie!" exclaimed Anne, "but I do wish she would not 'moo' like that, Mistress Stoddard. The British might hear her if they come up this far from shore."

" 'Tis only to remind me that it is time she was milked," said Mrs. Stoddard. "You can play about here, child, till I have finished."

Anne did not wander far. There was something else she wished to know, and when the bucket was filled with foamy, fragrant milk, of which Mrs. Stoddard bade the child drink, she said:

" 'Tis near a month since my father went. The Cary children also called after me that my father was a 'traitor'; is that an ill-seeming word?"

"The little oafs!" exclaimed Mrs. Stoddard, "and what else did they say?"

" 'Twill not make you dislike me, Mistress Stoddard?" questioned the child. "I honestly do not know why they should so beset me. But they called me 'beggar' as well, whatever that may be; though I'm sure I am not it, if it be an ill-seeming word."

Mrs. Stoddard had set down her milking-pail; Brownie was quietly feeding near by; there was no one to see, and she put her arm about the little girl and drew her near. It was the first outward show of tenderness that she had made toward the child, and as Anne felt the kindly pressure of her arm and looked up into the tender eyes her own face brightened.

"We'll sit here for a bit and rest, child," said Mrs. Stoddard, "and be sure I think only well of you. Thou art a dear child, and I will not have aught harm thee or make thee unhappy."

Anne drew a long breath, and snuggled closely to her good friend's side. A great load was lifted from her sad little heart, for since she had come to Provincetown she could remember but few kindly words, and to have Mistress Stoddard treat her with such loving kindness was happiness indeed. For a moment she forgot the taunts of the Cary children, and sat silent and smiling, her head resting against Mrs. Stoddard's shoulder. There was a peaceful little silence between the two, and then Anne spoke.

"I would wish to know what 'traitor' might mean, Mistress Stoddard?"

"Very like to 'spy,' " answered Mrs. Stodard. "The children meant that your father had told the British that they could find good harbor and provisions here. That, like a spy, he had opened the door of a friend's house for silver."

Anne sprang from the arm that had encircled her, her cheeks flushed and her eyes blazing. "Now!" she declared, "I *will* throw water upon them when I go to the spring! All that the bucket will hold I will splash upon them," and she made a fierce movement as if casting buckets full of wrath upon her enemies, "and sand!" she continued; "while they are wet with the water I will throw sand upon them. 'Tis worse to say things of my father than of me."

"Come here, child," said Mrs. Stoddard; "we will not let words like the Cary children speak trouble us. And you will remember, Anne, that I shall be ill-pleased if I hear of water-throwing at the spring. Come, now, we'll be going toward home."

Anne made no response, but walked quietly on beside her companion. When they reached the hilltop they paused again before going down the slope toward home.

"Look, Anne! Are not the fishing-boats all at anchor? What means it that the men are not about their fishing? We'd best hurry."

Captain Enos met them at the door. He gave Anne no word of greeting, but said to his wife, "The British tell us to keep ashore. They'll have no fishing. They know full well how easy 'tis for a good sloop to carry news up the harbor. They are well posted as to how such things are done."

"But what can we do if we cannot fish?" exclaimed Mrs. Stoddard. "'Tis well known that this sandy point is no place for gardens. We can scarce raise vegetables enough to know what they mean. And as for corn and wheat, every grain of them worth counting has to be bought from the other settlements and paid for in fish. If we do not fish how shall we eat?"

The captain shook his head. "Go about your play, child," he said, turning toward Anne, and the little girl walked slowly away toward a bunch of scrubby pine trees near which she had established a playhouse. She had built a cupboard of smooth chips, and here were gathered the shells she had brought from the beach, a wooden doll which her father had made her, and the pieces of a broken earthen-ware plate.

She took the doll from its narrow shelf and regard-ed it closely. Her father had made it with no small skill. Its round head was covered with curls carved in the soft wood; its eyes were colored with paint, and its mouth was red. The body was more clumsily made, but the arms and legs had joints, and the doll could sit up as erect as its small mistress. It wore one garment made of blue and white checked cotton. It was the only toy Anne Nelson had ever possessed, and it had seemed more her own because she had kept it in the little playhouse under the pines.

"Now, you can go up to the house and live with me," she said happily, "and now you shall have a true name. You shall be Martha Nelson now. I know my father would want you to be called Martha, if he knew that Mrs. Stoddard put her arm around me and called me a 'dear child,'" and Anne smiled at the remembrance.

She did not speak of her father before the Stoddards, but she could not have explained the rea-son for her silence. She had wondered much about him, and often watched the harbor yearningly, thinking that after all the old sloop might come sail-ing back, bringing the slender, silent man who had always smiled upon her, and praised her, and had told her that some day she should have a Maltese kitten, and a garden with blossoming trees and smooth paths. Anne did not forget him, and now as she regarded her wooden doll a great longing for a sight of his dear face made her forget everything, and she leaned her head against a little pine and cried silently. But as she cried the remembrance of the taunts of the Cary children came into her thoughts, and she dried her eyes.

" 'Tis near the hour when they go to the spring," she said, laying the doll carefully back in its former resting place. "I will but walk that way that they may not think me afraid of their ill-seeming words," and with her dark head more erect than usual, Anne made her way down the path, her brown feet sinking ankle-deep in the warm sand at every step.

The Cary children, a boy and a girl, both somewhat Anne's seniors, were already filling their buckets at the spring. Jimmie Starkweather was there, and a number of younger children ran shouting up and down the little stream which flowed from the spring across the road.

As Anne came near, Jimmie Starkweather called out: "Oh, Anne Nelson! The Indians from Truro are camping at Shankpainter's Pond. I've been over there, near enough to see them at work, this morning. My father says they'll be gone as soon as they see the British vessels. We'll not have time to buy moccasins if they go so quickly."

Anne's eyes rested for a moment upon Jimmie, but she did not speak. She could hear the Carys whispering as they dipped their buckets in the spring, and as she came nearer, their voices rose loudly: "Daughter of a spy! Beggar-child! Beggar-child!"

But their taunts vanished in splutterings and pleas for mercy; for at their first word Anne had sprung upon them like a young tiger. She had wrenched the bucket of water from the astonished boy and flung it in his face with such energy that he had toppled over backward, soused and whimpering; then she had turned upon his sister, sending handful after handful of sand into the face of that astonished child, until she fled from her, wailing for mercy.

But Anne pursued her relentlessly, and Captain Enos Stoddard, making his mournful way toward the shore, could hardly believe his own senses when he looked upon the scene—the Cary boy prostrate and humble, while his sister, pursued by Anne, prayed for Anne to stop the deluge of sand that seemed to fill the air about her.

"I'll not be called ill-seeming names!" shrieked Anne. "If thou sayest 'traitor' or 'spy' to me again I will do worse things to you!"

Captain Stoddard stood still for a moment. Then a slow smile crept over his weather-beaten face.

"Anne!" he called, and at the sound of his voice the child stopped instantly. "Come here," he said, and she approached slowly with hanging head. "Give me your hand, child," he said kindly, and the litle girl slipped her slender fingers into the big rough hand.

"So, Jimmie Starkweather, you'll stand by and see my little girl put upon, will you!" he exclaimed angrily. "I thought better than that of your father's son, to stand by and let a small girl be taunted with what she cannot help. It speaks ill for you."

"I had no time, sir," answered the boy sulkily; "she was upon them both in a second," and Jimmie's face brightened; "it was fine, sir, the way she sent yon lubber over," and he pointed a scornful finger toward the Cary boy, who was now slinking after his sister.

"Here, you Cary boy!" called the captain, "come back here and heed what I say to you. If I know of your opening your mouth with such talk again to my girl here," and he nodded toward Anne, "I'll deal with you myself. So look out for yourself."

"I'll see he keeps a civil tongue, sir," volunteered Jimmie, and Captain Enos nodded approvingly.

"Now, Anne, we'd best step up home," said the captain. "I expect Mistress Stoddard will not be pleased at this."

Anne clung close to the big hand but said no word.

"I am not angry, child," went on the captain. "I like your spirit. I do not believe in being put upon."

"But Mistress Stoddard told me I was not to throw water and sand," responded Anne, "and I forgot her commands. I fear she will not like me now," and remorseful tears dropped over the flushed little cheeks.

"There, there! Do not cry, Anne," comforted the captain; "I will tell her all about it. She will not blame you. You are my little girl now, and those Cary oafs will not dare open their mouths to plague you."

Mrs. Stoddard, looking toward the shore, could hardly credit what she saw—the captain, who but yesterday had declared that Anne should not stay under his roof, leading the child tenderly and smiling upon her!

"Heaven be thanked!" she murmured. "Enos has come to his senses. There'll be no more trouble about Anne staying."

CHAPTER III

ANNE'S SECRET

MRS. STODDARD said nothing to Anne of the trouble at the spring, and when Anne would have explained her part in it, her friend said quickly: "Captain Enos is not displeased with you, Anne. He thinks the Cary children not well taught at home, and says for you not to play with them," so that Anne had gone happily back to her playhouse, and told "Martha" that there was no one so good as Mistress and Captain Stoddard, "except my dear father," the little girl had added loyally.

"Now, Martha, you must be a good and quiet child," she advised, "for after this you will live in the house with me. You can come out here to play with me, but every night you are to sleep in my bed; and it may be, Mistress Stoddard will let you rest in the kitchen now and then, and you may go with me over the pasture hill to see Brownie."

The big British ships lay quietly at anchor for several days. The men came ashore in boatloads, washed their clothes at the spring, bought such provisions as the little settlement could offer, and wandered about the shore. The citizens treated them not uncivilly, for since the men of Provincetown were unable to make any resistance to those they felt to be their country's foes, they knew it to be best to be silent and accept the authority they had not the strength to defy. So the fishing-boats swung at anchor in the harbor, and the men lingered about the landing, or fished for plaice fish and sole from their dories near shore.

"We'll be poor indeed when frost comes," complained Mrs. Stoddard; "my molasses keg is near empty now, and the meal barrel not half full. If those Britishers do not soon leave the harbor so that the men can get back to the fishing, this place will know hunger, for our larder is no poorer than our neighbors'."

"Yes," agreed Captain Enos, "the whole coast is feeling the king's displeasure because we will not pay him taxes to fill his pockets, and make slaves of us. I wish we had some news of our Boston friends. The Freemans are well to do, but with Boston beset on all sides with British soldiers they may be hard pressed."

" 'Twill come to worse yet, be sure," predicted Mrs. Stoddard gloomily.

It was but a few days after this when with joyful songs the British sailors made ready to sail, and on a bright July morning the vessels, taking advantage of a fair wind, bent their sails and skimmed away up the coast.

"They are bound for Boston," declared Captain Enos, "and 'tis soon enough they'll be back again. The Boston folk will not let them come to anchor, I'll be bound."

Hardly had the ships got under headway before the fishermen were rowing out to their sailboats, and soon the little fleet was under sail bound off Race Point toward the fishing grounds.

"Now, Anne, you had best go after Brownie and bring her back to her old pasture. I like not the long tramp morning and night to milk the creature," said Mrs. Stoddard, and she watched Anne, with the wooden doll clasped in her arm, go obediently off on her errand.

A little smile crept over her face as she stood in the doorway. "Captain Enos would like well that Anne be called Anne Stoddard," she said aloud; "he begins to recall good traits in her father, and to think no other child in the settlement has the spirit that our girl has. And I am well pleased that it is so," she concluded with a little sigh, "for there will be poor days ahead for us to bear, and had the captain not changed his mind about Anne I should indeed have had hard work to manage," and she turned back to her simple household tasks.

Anne went slowly up the sandy slope, stopping here and there to see if the beach plums showed any signs of ripening, and turning now and then to see if she could pick out Captain Enos's sail among the boats going swiftly out toward the open sea.

As she came in sight of the little grove of maples her quick eyes saw a man moving among them. Brownie was quietly feeding, evidently undisturbed. Anne stopped, holding Martha very tightly, her eyes fixed upon the moving figure. She was not afraid, but she wondered who it was, for she thought that every man in the settlement had gone to the fishing grounds. As she looked, something familiar in the man's movements sent her running toward the grove.

"It is my father. I know it is my father," she whispered to herself. As she came down the slope the man evidently saw her, for he came out from the wood a little as if waiting for her.

"Anne, Anne!" he exclaimed, as she came near, and in a moment his arm was around her and he was clasping her close.

"Come back in the wood, dear child," he said. "And you have not forgotten your father?"

Anne smiled up at him happily. "I could never do that," she responded. "See, here is my doll. Her name is Martha Stoddard Nelson."

"An excellent name," declared the man smilingly. "How neat and rosy you look, Anne! You look as if you had fared well. Be they kind to you?"

"Oh, yes, father. They say now that I am their little girl. But I am not," and Anne shook her head smilingly. "I am my own father's little girl; though I like them well," she added.

The two were seated on a grassy hummock where no eye could see them; but from time to time John Nelson looked about furtively as if expecting some one to appear.

"You are not a 'traitor' or a 'spy,' are you, father?" questioned the child. "When the Cary children did say so I chased them from the spring, and Captain Enos said I did well. But I did think you lost at sea, father!"

The man shook his head. "Try and remember what I tell you, child, that you may know your father for an honest man. The day I left harbor on my fishing trip I was run down by one of those British vessels. The sloop sank, and they threw me a rope and pulled me on board. It was rare sport for their sailors to see me struggle for my very life." The man stopped and his face grew very grave and stern. "They they said they were coming into Cape Cod Harbor, and that I should be their pilot. They said they would make a good bonfire of the shanties of the settlement. And then, child, I misled them. I laughed and said, ' 'Tis a settlement of good Royalists if ever there was one.' They would scarce believe me. But they came into harbor, and when the men proved civil and refused them nothing, then they credited what I said. But they told me they were bound for Dorchester Harbor, and there they would make a good English soldier of me. I said nothing, but this morning, in the confusion of making sail, I slipped overboard and swam ashore, bound that I would have a look at my girl and know her safe and well."

"And now, father, shall we go back and live in the little house by the shore? Mistress Stoddard has kept our things safely, and she has taught me many useful things," said Anne proudly.

"No, child. For me to stay in this settlement would bring trouble upon it. Those ships will return here, and if I were found among the men here, then, indeed, would their anger be great. They must think me drowned, else they would indeed make a bonfire of every house along the shore."

"But what will you do, father? You must stay with me now."

"No, dear child. I must make my way up the cape to the settlements and join the Americans. My eyes are opened: 'tis right that they should protect their homes. I will have some information for them, and I no longer have any place here. The Stoddards are good to you, Anne? They task thee not beyond thy strength? and they speak pleasantly to thee?"

"They are ever kind, father; they do smile on me, and Captain Enos does always give me the best piece of fish at table; and he told the Cary children that I was his little girl, and that I was not to be plagued. But he is not my own father," answered Anne, "and if you must go up the cape I will go with you. The nights are warm and pleasant, and I shall like well to sleep out-of-doors with the stars shining down on us. And if you go with the Americans I will go too. They will not mind one little girl!"

Her father smoothed the dark hair tenderly and smiled at the eager, upturned face.

"You love me, Anne, and I'll not forget that I have a dear, brave daughter waiting for me. I'll be the braver and the better man remembering. But you cannot go with me. I shall be scant fed and footsore for many a long day, and I will not let you bear any hardship I can keep from you. It will be a joy to me to know you safe with Mistress Stoddard; and if I live they shall be repaid for all they do for you. They are indeed kind to you?" he again questioned anxiously.

"They are indeed," responded Anne, seriously.

"Now I must begin my journey, Anne. And do not say that you have seen me. Keep in your heart all I have told you. I shall come for you when I can. But you are to be happy and not think of me as in danger. A brave man is always quite safe, and I wish you to believe that your father is a brave man, Anne."

"Am I not to tell Mistress Stoddard?"

"Tell no one, Anne. Remember. Promise me that when they speak of me as drowned you will say no word!"

"I will not speak, father. But if they do say 'traitor' or 'spy' I am not to bear it. Captain Enos said I need not."

A little smile came over the man's face and he nodded silently. Then he kissed his little daughter and again promising that it should not be long before he would come for her, he turned and made his way through the wood, and soon Anne could no longer see him.

For a long time the little girl sat silent and sorrowful where he had left her. She had forgotten all about the little brown cow; her wooden doll lay neglected on the grass beside her. But after a little she remembered the errand on which she had been sent, and, picking Martha up, started off to drive Brownie back to the pasture near home.

Anne was so quiet that day that at night Mrs. Stoddard questioned her anxiously. "Have those Cary children been saying hateful words to you again, child?" she asked.

"No, I have not been to the spring," answered Anne.

"Has Jimmie Starkweather been telling thee more foolish tales of a big wolf that comes prowling about at night?" continued Mrs. Stoddard.

"Oh, no, Mistress Stoddard. And indeed I do not think Jimmie Starkweather would frighten me. You know his father has seen the wolf. 'Twas near Blackwater Pond."

"Then, child, I fear you are ill. Your face is flushed and you left your porridge untasted. Would you like it better if I put a spoonful of molasses over it?"

Anne nodded soberly. Molasses was not to be refused, even if she must live without her brave father; and so she ate her porridge, and Mrs. Stoddard patted her on the shoulder, and told her that the beach-plums would soon be ripening and then she should have a pie, sweet and crusty. And if the captain did well at the fishing, and the British ships kept their distance, she should have some barley sugar, a great treat in those days.

"We'll be getting you some sort of foot-gear before long, too," promised Mrs. Stoddard. "I have enough wool yarn in the house to knit you a good pair of warm stockings. 'Tis an ugly gray; I wish I could plan some sort of dye for it to make it a prettier color."

"But I like gray," said Anne. "Last winter my feet were cold, and ached with the chilblains. My father knew not how to get stockings for me, and cut down his own, but they were hard to wear."

"I should say so!" said Mrs. Stoddard; "a man is a poor manager when it comes to fending for children's clothes. 'Tis well I am provided with some warm garments. When the frost comes you shall learn to knit, Anne; and if we be in good fortune you shall do a sampler," and Anne, comforted and somewhat consoled by all these pleasant plans for her future happiness, went to sleep that night with the wooden doll closely clasped in her arms, wishing her father might know how good Mistress Stoddard was to her.

CHAPTER IV

ANNE AND THE WOLF

"A PIE of beach-plums, sweet and crusty," Anne repeated to herself the next day as she carried Martha out to the playhouse, and rearranged her bits of crockery, and looked off across the harbor.

"I do wish they would ripen speedily," she said aloud. "Indeed those I tasted of yesterday had a pleasant flavor, and I am sure Mistress Stoddard would be well pleased if I could bring home enough for a pie. I will take the small brown basket and follow the upper path, for the plum bushes grow thickly there," and Martha was carefully settled in her accustomed place, and Anne ran to the house for the brown basket, and in a few moments was following a sandy path which led toward the salt meadows.

She stopped often to pick the yellowing beach-plums, and now and then tasted one hopefully, expecting to find the sweet pungent flavor which the children so well loved, but only once or twice did she discover any sign of ripeness.

"I'll cross the upper marsh," she decided; "'tis not so shaded there, and the sun lies warm till late in the day, and the plums are sure to be sweeter. I hope my father finds many to eat along his journey. I wish I had told him that it was best for me to go with him. We could have made little fires at night and cooked a fish, and, with berries to eat, it would not have been unpleasant."

The July sun beat warmly down, but a little breath of air from the sea moved steadily across the marshes filled with many pleasant odors. Here and there big bunches of marsh rosemary made spots of soft violet upon the brown grass, and now and then little flocks of sand-peeps rose from the ground and fluttered noisily away. But there was a pleasant midsummer stillness in the air, and by the time Anne had crossed the marsh and reached the shade of a low-growing oak tree she began to feel tired and content to rest a time before continuing her search for ripe beach-plums.

"I wish I had put Martha in the basket," she thought as she leaned comfortably back against the scrubby trunk of the little tree; "then I could have something to talk to." But she had not much time to regret her playmate, for in a second her eyes had closed and she was fast asleep. There was a movement in the bushes behind her, a breaking of twigs, a soft fall of padded feet, but she did not awaken.

A big animal with a soft, gray coat of fur, with sharp nose and ears alertly pointed, came out from the woods, sniffed the soft air cautiously, and turned his head warily toward the oak tree. The creature was evidently not alarmed at what he saw there, for he approached the sleeping child gently, made a noiseless circle about her, and then settled down at her feet, much as a big dog might have done. His nose rested upon his paws and his sharp eyes were upon the sleeping child.

In a little while Anne awoke. She had dreamed that Jimmie Starkweather had led a beautiful, big gray animal to Mistress Stoddard's door, and told her that it was a wolf that he had tamed; so when she opened her eyes and saw the animal so near her she did not jump with surprise, but she said softly, "Wolf!"

The creature sprang to its feet at the sound of her voice, and moved off a few paces, and then turned and looked over its shoulder at Anne.

"Wolf!" Anne repeated, brushing her hair from her eyes and pulling her sunbonnet over her head. Then she reached out for the plum basket, and stood up. Still the animal had not moved.

"I do believe it is tame," thought Anne, and she made a step toward her visitor, but the gray wolf no longer hesitated, and with a bound it was off on a run across the marsh, and soon disappeared behind a clump of bushes.

"I wish it had stayed," Anne said aloud, for there had been nothing to make her afraid of wild creatures, and Jimmie's stories of a big wolf ranging about the outskirts of the settlement had not suggested to her that a wolf was any thing which would do her harm, and she continued her search for beach-plums, her mind filled with the thought of many pleasant things.

"I do think, Mistress Stoddard, that I have plums enough for a pie," she exclaimed, as she reached the kitchen door and held up her basket for Mistress Stoddard's inspection.

" 'Twill take a good measure of molasses, I fear," declared Mrs. Stoddard, "but you shall have the pie, dear child. 'Twill please Captain Enos mightily to have a pie for his supper when he gets in from the fishing; and I'll tell him 'twas Anne who gathered the plums," and she nodded smilingly at the little girl.

"And what think you has happened at the spring this morning?" she went on, taking the basket from Anne, who followed her into the neat little kitchen. "Jimmie Starkweather and his father near captured a big gray wolf. The creature walked up to the spring to drink as meek as a calf, and Mr. Starkweather ran for his axe to kill it, but 'twas off in a second."

"But why should he kill it?" exclaimed Anne. "I'm sure 'tis a good wolf. 'Twas no harm for it to drink from the spring."

"But a wolf is a dangerous beast," replied Mrs. Stoddard; "the men-folk will take some way to capture it."

Anne felt the tears very near her eyes. To her, the gray wolf had not seemed dangerous. It had looked kindly upon her, and she had already resolved that if it ever were possible she would like to stroke its soft fur.

"Couldn't the wolf be tamed?" she questioned. "I went to sleep near the marsh this morning and dreamed that Jimmie Starkweather had a tame wolf." But for some reason, which Anne herself could not have explained, she did not tell her good friend of the wild creature which had come so near to her when she slept, and toward whom she had so friendly a feeling, and Mrs. Stoddard, busy with her preparations for pie-making, did not speak further of the wolf.

There was a good catch of fish that day, and Captain Enos came home smiling and well pleased.

"If we could hope that the British ships would keep out of harbor we could look forward to some comfort," he said, "but Starkweather had news from an Ipswich fisherman that the 'Somerset' was cruising down the cape, and like as not she'll anchor off the village some morning. And from what we hear, her sailors find it good sport to lay hands on what they see."

The appearance of the beach-plum pie, warm from the oven, turned the captain's thoughts to more pleasant subjects. " 'Tis a clever child to find ripe beach-plums in July," he said, as he cut Anne a liberal piece, "and a bit of tartness gives it an excellent flavor. Well, well, it is surely a pleasant thing to have a little maid in the house," and he nodded kindly toward Anne.

After supper when Anne had gone up to her little chamber under the eaves, and Captain Enos and Mrs. Stoddard were sitting upon their front door-step enjoying the cool of the evening, Captain Enos said:

"Martha, Anne calls you Mistress Stoddard, does she not?"

"Always," answered his wife. "She is a most thoughtful and respectful child. Never does she speak of thee, Enos, except to say 'Captain.' She has been in the house for over two months now, and I see no fault in her."

"A quick temper," responded Captain Enos, but his tone was not that of a person who had discovered a fault. Indeed he smiled as he spoke, remembering the flight of the Cary children.

"I would like well to have the little maid feel that we were pleased with her," continued the captain slowly. "If she felt like calling me 'Father' and you 'Mother,' I should see no harm in it, and perhaps 'twould be well to have her name put on the town records as bearing our name, Anne Stoddard?" and Captain Enos regarded his wife questioningly.

"It is what I have been wishing for, Enos!" exclaimed Mrs. Stoddard, "but maybe 'twere better for the child to call us 'Uncle' and 'Aunt.' She does not yet forget her own father, you see, and she might feel 'twere not right to give another his name."

Captain Enos nodded approvingly. "A good and loyal heart she has, I know," he answered, "and 'twill be better indeed not to puzzle the little maid. We'll be 'Uncle' and 'Aunt' to her then, Martha; and as for her name on the town records, perhaps we'll let the matter rest till Anne is old enough to choose for herself. If the British keep on harrying us it may well be that we fisherfolk will have to go further up the coast for safety."

"And desert Provincetown?" exclaimed Mrs. Stoddard, "the place where your father and mine, Enos, were born and died, and their fathers before them. No—we'll not search for safety at such a price. I doubt if I could live in those shut-in places such as I hear the upper landings are."

Captain Enos chuckled approvingly. "I knew well what you would say to that, Martha," he replied, "and now we must get our sleep, for the tide serves early to-morrow morning, and I must make the best of these good days."

"Captain Enos was well pleased with the pie, Anne," said Mrs. Stoddard the next morning, as the little girl stood beside her, carefully wiping the heavy ironware. "And what does thee think! The captain loves thee so well, child, that it would please him to have thee call him Uncle Enos. That is kind of him, is it not, Anne?" and Mistress Stoddard smiled down at the eager little face at her elbow.

"It is indeed, Mistress Stoddard," replied Anne happily; "shall I begin to-night?"

"Yes, child, and I shall like it well if you call me 'Aunt'; 'twill seem nearer than 'Mistress Stoddard,' and you are same as our own child now."

Anne's dark eyes looked up earnestly into Mistress Stoddard's kind face. "But I am my father's little girl, too," she said.

"Of course you are," answered her friend. "Captain Enos and I are not asking you to forget your father, child. No doubt he did his best for you, but you are to care for us, too."

"But I do, Aunt Martha; I love you well," said Anne, so naturally that Mrs. Stoddard stopped her work long enough to give her a kiss and to say, "There, child, now we are all settled. 'Twill please your Uncle Enos well."

As soon as the few dishes were set away Anne wandered down the hill toward the spring. She no longer feared the Cary children, and she hoped to see some of the Starkweather family and hear more of the gray wolf, and at the spring she found Jimmie with two wooden buckets filled and ready for him to carry home to his waiting mother.

"You missed the great sight yesterday, Anne," he said, as she approached the spring. "What think you! A wolf as big as a calf walked boldly up and drank, right where I stand."

" 'Twas not as big as a calf," declared Anne; " and why should you seek to kill a wild creature who wants but a drink? 'Tis not a bad wolf."

Jimmie looked at her in surprise, his gray eyes widening and shining in wonder. "All wolves are bad," he declared. "This same gray wolf walked off with Widow Bett's plumpest hen and devoured it before her very eyes."

"Well, the poor creature was hungry. We eat plump hens, when we can get them," answered Anne.

Jimmie laughed good-naturedly. "Wait till you see the beast, Anne," he answered. "Its eyes shine like black water, and its teeth show like pointed rocks.

You'd not stand up for it so boldly if you had but seen it."

Anne made no answer; she was not even tempted to tell Jimmie that she had seen the animal, had been almost within arm's reach of it.

"I must be going," she said, "but do not harm the wolf, Jimmie," and she looked at the boy pleadingly; "perhaps it knows no better than to take food when it is hungry."

"I'd like its skin for a coat," the boy answered, "but 'tis a wise beast and knows well how to take care of itself. It's miles away by this time," and picking up the buckets he started toward home, and Anne turned away from the spring and walked toward the little pasture where Brownie fed in safety.

She stopped to speak to the little brown cow and to give her a handful of tender grass, and then wandered down the slope and along the edge of the marsh.

"Maybe 'twill come again," she thought, as she reached the little oak tree and sat down where she had slept the day before. "Perhaps if I sit very still it will come out again. I'm sure 'tis not an unfriendly beast."

The little girl sat very still; she did not feel sleepy or tired, and her dark eyes scanned the marsh hopefully, but as the summer morning drifted toward noon she began to realize that her watch was in vain.

"I s'pose Jimmie Starkweather was right, and the gray wolf is miles away," she thought, as she decided that she must leave the shadow of the oak and hurry toward home so that Aunt Martha would not be anxious about her.

"I wish the wolf knew I liked him," the little girl said aloud, as she turned her face toward home. "I would not chase him away from the spring, and I would not want his gray fur for a coat," and Anne's face was very sober, as she sent a lingering look along the thick-growing woods that bordered the marsh. She often thought of the wolf, but she never saw it again.

CHAPTER V

SCARLET STOCKINGS

"Good news from Truro, Captain Enos," said Joseph Starkweather, one morning in August, as the two neighbors met at the boat landing. "There'll be good hope for American freedom if all our settlements show as much wit and courage."

"And what have Truro men done?" demanded Captain Enos. "They are mostly of the same blood as our Provincetown folks, and would naturally be of some wit."

Joseph Starkweather's eyes brightened and twinkled at his neighbor's answer.

" 'Twas the sand-hills helped them," he answered. "You know the little valleys between the row of sand-hills near the shore? Well, the British fleet made anchorage off there some days since, and the Truro men had no mind for them to land and spy out how few there were. So they gathered in one of those little valleys and, carrying smooth poles to look like muskets, they marched out in regular file like soldiers over the sand-hill; then down they went through the opposite depression and around the hill and back, and then up they came again, constantly marching; and the British, who could be seen getting boats ready to land, thought better of it. They believed that an immense force of American soldiers had assembled, and the ships hoisted sail and made off. 'Twas good work."

"Indeed it was," responded Captain Enos. "I could wish that we of this settlement were not so at the mercy of the British. Our harbor is too good. It draws them like a magnet. I do think three thousand ships might find safe anchorage here, and Captain Enos turned an admiring look out across the beautiful harbor.

"Have you any news of John Nelson?" questioned Joseph Starkweather.

"How could there be news of a man whose boat sunk under him well off Race Point in a southerly gale?" responded Captain Stoddard.

Joseph approached a step nearer his companion and said: "He was on one of the British ships, Enos; he was seen there, and now news comes by way of a Nerwburyport fisherman that 'twas no fault of John Nelson's. The Britishers ran down his boat and took him on board their ship, and the news goes that when the fleet anchored off here Nelson escaped; swam ashore in the night, the story goes, and made his way to Wellfleet and joined the Americans at Dorchester who are ready to resist the British if need be."

Captain Enos's face brightened as he listened. "That is indeed good news!" he said. "I am glad for our little maid's sake that her father is known to be a loyal man. But 'tis strange he did not seek to see Anne," he continued thoughtfully.

"John Nelson loved the little maid well," declared Joseph Starkweather. "He had but poor luck here, but he did his best. The Newburyport man tells that the British are in great anger at his escape, and vow that the settlement here shall pay well for it when they make harbor here again."

"We have no arms to defend the harbor. 'Tis hard work to rest quiet here," said Captain Enos; "but it is great news to know that our little maid's father is a loyal man. We like the child well."

" 'Twas I sent Anne to your house, Enos," responded Joseph. "My own is so full that I dared not ask Mistress Starkweather to take the child in; and I knew your wife for a kind-hearted woman."

"It was a good thought, Joseph," responded the captain, "and Anne seems well content with us. She has her playhouse under the trees, and amuses herself without making trouble. She is a helpful little maid, too, saving Mistress Stoddard many a step. I must be going toward home. There was an excellent chowder planned for my dinner, and Martha will rejoice at the news from Truro," and the captain hurried toward home.

Half-way up the hill he saw Anne, coming to meet him. "Uncle Enos! Uncle Enos!" she called, "Brownie is lost! Indeed she is. All the morning have I gone up and down the pasture, calling her name and looking everywhere for her, and she is not to be found."

"Well, well!" responded Captain Enos; "'tis sure the Britishers have not stolen her, for there is not one of their craft in sight. The cow is probably feeding somewhere about; we'll find her safe in some good pasturage. Is the chowder steaming hot and waiting?"

"Yes, Uncle Enos," replied Anne, slipping her hand into the captain's, "but Aunt Martha is greatly concerned about Brownie. She fears the Indians may have driven her off."

"We'll cruise about a little after dinner," answered the captain. "I don't like to think that the Indians would show themselves unfriendly just now," and his pleasant face grew stern and serious.

But his appetite for the chowder was excellent, and when he started out to search for Brownie he was sure that he would find her near the marsh or perhaps in the maple grove further on, where the cattle sometimes wandered.

"Now, Anne, I have an errand for you to do," said Mrs. Stoddard, as the captain started on his search. "I've just remembered that the Starkweather children had good stockings last year of crimson yarn. Now it may be that Mrs. Starkweather has more on hand, and that I could exchange my gray, as she has stout boys to wear gray stockings, for her scarlet yarn; and then we'll take up some stockings for you."

Anne's face brightened. "I should well like some scarlet stockings," she said.

"I mean you to be warmly clad come frost," said Mrs. Stoddard. "Now see that you do the errand well. Ask Mrs. Starkweather, first of all, if she be in good health. It is not seemly to be too earnest in asking a favor. Then say that Mistress Stoddard has enough excellent gray yarn for two pair of long stockings, and that she would take it as a kindness if Mistress Starkweather would take it in exchange for scarlet yarn."

"Yes, Aunt Martha, I will surely remember," and Anne started off happily.

As she passed the spring a shrill voice called her name and she turned to see Amanda Cary, half hidden behind a small savin.

"Come and play," called Amanda. "I am not angry if you did chase me. My mother says you knew no better!"

Anne listened in amazement. Knew no better! Had not Captain Enos approved of her defense of herself, and were not the Cary children the first to begin trouble with her! So Anne shook her head and walked sedately on.

"Come and play," repeated the shrill voice. "My brother and Jimmie Starkweather are gone looking for our cow, and I have no one to play with."

"Is your cow lost, too?" exclaimed Anne, quite forgetting Amanda's unkindness in this common ill-fortune.

Amanda now came out from behind the savin tree; a small, thin-faced child, with light eyes, sandy hair and freckles.

"Yes, and we think the Indians have driven them off. For the Starkweathers' cow is not to be found. 'Twill be a sad loss, my mother says; for it will leave but three cows in the town."

"But they may be found," insisted Anne. "My Uncle Enos has gone now to look for Brownie."

"'Uncle Enos'!" repeated Amanda scornfully. "He's not your uncle. You are a waif. My mother said so, and waifs do not have uncles or fathers or anybody."

"I am no waif, for I have a father, and my Uncle Enos will tell your mother not to say such words of me!" declared Anne boldly, but she felt a lump in her throat and wished very much that she had not stopped to talk with Amanda.

"I don't see why you get angry so quick," said Amanda. "You get angry at everything. I'd just as soon play with you, if you are a waif."

"I wouldn't play with you anyway," said Anne; "I have an errand to do, and if I had not I would rather never play than play with such a hateful, ill-speaking child as you are," and Anne hurried on her way toward the Starkweathers' low-built, weather-beaten house near the shore.

"I shall be glad indeed to get rid of some of my scarlet yarn," declared Mrs. Starkweather, "and you can take home a skein or two of it and tell Mistress Stoddard that her little girl does an errand very prettily. I could wish my boys were as well-mannered."

Anne smiled, well pleased at the pleasant words.

"Uncle Enos says there is no better boy than Jimmie," she responded. "He says he is a smart and honest lad,—a 'real Starkweather,' he calls him," she responded.

"Does he so?" and the woman's thin face flushed with pleasure at this praise of her eldest son. "Well, we do prize Jimmie, and 'tis good news to know him well thought of, and you are a kindly little maid to speak such pleasant words. Mistress Stoddard is lucky indeed to have you."

"I call her Aunt Martha now," said Anne, feeling that Mrs. Starkweather was nearly as kind as Mrs. Stoddard, and quite forgetting the trouble of Brownie's loss or of Amanda's teasing in the good woman's pleasantness.

"That is well," replied Mrs. Starkweather. "You will bring her much happiness, I can well see. I could wish you had come to me, child, when your father went; but the Stoddards can do better for you."

"Should I have called you 'Aunt'?" Anne asked a little wistfully.

"Indeed you should, and you may now if Mistress Stoddard be willing. Say to her that I'd like well to be Aunt Starkweather to her little maid."

So Anne, with her bundle of scarlet yarn, started toward home, much happier than when she had rapped at Mrs. Starkweather's door.

Amanda was still sitting at the spring. "Anne," she called shrilly, "may I go up to your house and play with you?"

Anne shook her head, and without a backward look at the child by the spring kept on her way toward home. She had much to tell her Aunt Martha, who listened, well pleased at her neighbor's kind words.

"And Amanda Cary said that their cow was lost, and the Starkweathers' cow, too. Amos Cary and

Jimmie are off searching for them now, and do fear the Indians have driven them off," said Anne.

" 'Twill be bad fortune indeed if that be true, replied Mrs. Stoddard, "for we are not as well provisioned for the winter as usual, and it would be a worrisome thing to have the Indians bothering us on shore and the British to fear at sea. But I'll take up your stockings to-day, Anne. The yarn is a handsome color, and well spun."

"I think I will not leave Martha at the playhouse after this," said Anne thoughtfully; "something might happen to her."

Mrs. Stoddard nodded approvingly, and Anne brought the wooden doll in.

"Like as not our Uncle Enos will make you a wooden chair for the doll when the evenings get longer," said Mrs. Stoddard. "He's clever with his knife, and 'twill give him something to busy his hands with. I'll call his attention to the doll."

"My!" exclaimed Anne, "I do think an aunt and uncle are nice to have. And a father is too," she added quickly, for she could not bear that any one should think that she had forgotten her own father.

"Yes, indeed, child; and there's good news of your own father. He was on the British ship and escaped and made his way to Wellfleet to join the American soldiers."

"Oh, Aunt Martha!" and the little girl sprang up from her little stool and grasped her good friend's gown with eager hands, and then told her the story of her father's visit. "But I could not tell it before," she said.

"Indeed you are a loyal little maid," replied Mrs. Stoddard approvingly, "and you must always keep a promise, but see to it that you promise nothing quickly. I think the better of John Nelson that he took great risk to make sure his little daughter was safe and well cared for. The captain will think it good news, too."

"My father will come back some day," declared Anne, and Mrs. Stoddard agreed cheerfully.

"To be sure he will," she said, "but do not think of that too much, dear child. See, I have the stitches all cast on, and your scarlet stockings are really begun."

CHAPTER VI

CAPTURED BY INDIANS

THE more Anne thought about Brownie the more fearful she became that some harm had befallen the pretty brown cow.

"Her foot may have caught in those twisted roots on the hill," thought the little girl, "or perhaps the Indians have fastened her in the woods. I do believe I could find her, and save Uncle Enos the trouble," and the more Anne thought of it the more eager she became to search for Brownie; and, on the day that the scarlet stockings were begun, Anne resolved to walk up the hill and look about for the missing cow.

As she trudged along she thought of many things, of the gray wolf, which had disappeared completely, having probably made its way up the cape to better hunting grounds; and she thought a great deal about her father, and of the day he had come to tell her of his safety. But Anne did not think much about the Indians. The cape settlements had been on friendly terms with the Chatham Indians for some time, and the people of Provincetown were more in peril from the freebooters of the sea than from Indians.

Anne had climbed the hill, passed the grove of scrubby pines, and stood looking across the sand-dunes toward the open sea. She had looked carefully for Brownie, but there was no trace of her. But Anne was sure that, at the edge of the pine woods, some creature had been near her. She had lived out-of-doors so much that her ears were quick to distinguish any sound. At first she had wondered if it might not be the wolf, and, as she stood looking across the sand, she almost hoped that it might be. "Perhaps I could tame it and have it live at our house," she thought, and then remembered what Aunt Martha had said: that it would be a hard winter, "and wolves eat a good deal, I suppose," decided Anne, "so 'twill not be wise to tame it."

Had she looked behind her she would not have felt so secure. An Indian woman had been following Anne, and was now within arm's reach of her. And Anne had just come to her decision in regard to the wolf, when a blanket fell over her head, was quickly twisted about her, and she felt herself lifted from the ground. Then she heard a chatter of voices in a strange tongue, and realized that she was being carried away from the pine woods. She tried to free herself from the blanket, and tried to call out; but she could not move, and her voice made only a muffled sound. She heard a laugh from the squaw who was carrying her so easily, and in a moment felt herself dropped on the soft sand, and held down firmly for a moment. Then she lay quietly. She knew, though she could not see, that a canoe was being launched. There was talk among a number of people near her, and then she was lifted and put into the canoe, and again firmly held by a strong arm. Then came the smooth dip of paddles, and Anne knew that she was being taken away from home, and she felt the tears on her cheeks. She did not try to scream again, for there had been a rough twist of the blanket about her head when she cried out before, and she was held too firmly to struggle. She could hear the guttural voices of the Indians, and, after what seemed a long time, she realized that her captors were making a landing. She was again dropped on sand, and now the blanket was unwound and Anne stood up. She found herself facing three Indian women. Two of them frowned at her, but the younger smiled and nodded, and patted Anne's shoulder.

The two elder squaws began to talk rapidly, but the one who stood beside Anne remained silent. The canoe was lifted from the beach by the two, as they talked, and carried up toward the rough pasture-land. Anne's companion took her by the hand and led her after the others.

A BLANKET FELL OVER HER HEAD

"I want to go right home," Anne announced. "You must take me right back to Captain Stoddard's." The young squaw shook her head, still smiling, and Anne realized that her companion could not understand what she said. The little girl stopped short, and then the smile faded from the squaw's face; she gave her an ugly twitch forward, and when Anne still refused to move a stinging blow on the cheek followed. Anne began to cry bitterly. She was now thoroughly frightened, and began to wonder what would become of her.

The squaws hid the canoe carefully, covering it up with vines and brush, and then started along the shore. Anne and her companion now kept close to the other two. And the three squaws talked together. Now and then they would stop, and shading their eyes with one hand, look seaward as if watching for some expected boat, but none appeared. Anne's bare feet began to ache. She believed they would be blistered, but the women paid no attention to her. Anne knew that they were very near the Truro beach. She could see the big waves dashing up in a long curving line, and as they came round a high cliff of sand they came suddenly upon a big fishing-boat drawn up on the beach. Two sailors stood by it. In an instant the squaws had turned to flee, dragging Anne with them.

But she screamed, and threw herself down on the sand. The sailors came running toward them, and the Indian women fled.

"It's a white child," exclaimed one of the men, picking Anne up, and wiping her face with a big soft handkerchief. "What were they doing with you, child?" And leaning against his friendly arm, Anne told her story, and showed her bruised feet.

" 'Tis lucky for you we put ashore," said the man. "We'll take you home, little maid, safe and sound."

"You are not from Provincetown?" Anne ventured to ask, looking up in the kind blue eyes.

"We are good English sailors, my girl," the other man answered her question, "and we borrowed this boat from a settler up shore to get fish for His Majesty's ship 'Somerset'; but we'll take you safe home, never fear."

The blue-eyed man lifted Anne into the boat, and the two men were soon pulling strongly at the oars.

"'Tis a stiff pull to Provincetown, but the tide's with us, William," said the last speaker.

Anne sat very quiet. She was wondering if Aunt Martha had missed her, and if Uncle Enos would blame her for having wandered to the outer beach. She looked up to see the sailor whom his companion called "William" smiling at her.

"Do not be afraid," he said kindly; "the folks at home will be glad to see you, and you'll not be scolded."

Anne tried to smile back. She wanted to ask him if he had any little girls of his own; but she remembered that he was an Englishman, and decided that it was best not to say anything.

"Can you walk across the pasture if we set you ashore near here?" asked the sailor, when they had reached the smooth beach near where Anne had been seized by the Indians. "You'll not be troubled again, and we cannot well round the point to-night."

"I can get home from here. I see the pine woods," Anne agreed, and the men ran the boat well up on the beach, and William lifted her out.

" 'Tis hard for those tender feet," he said, "but be quick as you can. My name is William Trull, if your folks ask who 'twas that fetched you home, and my mate's name here is Richard Jones."

"Thank you; my name is Anne Nelson," Anne replied.

She turned back and waved her hand to them when she had reached the land above the shore, and saw them push off their boat and row away. It was very hard now to walk over the rough ground, and Anne felt very tired and unhappy. She kept steadily on, and was soon in sight of home. Mistress Stoddard and Captain Enos were both standing in the doorway looking anxiously toward her.

"Well, well, Anne, and do you think you should stay away like this? And what has become of your sunbonnet?" questioned Mrs. Stoddard.

"Indians!" wailed Anne. "Indian women, Aunt Martha! They carried me off," and, with Mrs. Stoddard's arm about her, and Captain Enos listening in angry amazement, Anne told the story of her adventure.

"'Twas an evil thing!" declared the captain. "I'm thankful the English sailors were on shore. I'll remember their names."

Mrs. Stoddard bathed the tired feet, and Anne was quite hungry enough to relish the hot corn bread, even though she had no milk to drink with it.

"We must be careful about letting the child wander about alone," Captain Enos said, after Anne was safe in bed that night. " 'Twould be ill-fortune indeed if harm befell her."

"I'll keep her more at home," replied Mrs. Stoddard. "She is to begin knitting now, and that will give her amusement indoors."

" 'Tis said that English soldiers are coming into Boston by land and sea," said Captain Enos. "We Provincetown people are exempt from military service, but we are loyal to the American forces, and some of us think the time is near when we must let you women stay here by yourselves," and Captain Enos looked at his wife questioningly.

"We'd do our best, Enos, be sure of that," she answered bravely, "and I'd have Anne for company, if you're needed in Boston."

"If we stood any chance of getting there," complained Captain Enos, "without the Britishers making us prisoners. No boat gets by them, I'm told."

"Talk no more of it to-night, Enos. Mayhap things may be settled soon, and these unhappy days well over," and Mistress Stoddard stepped to the door and looked out on the peaceful little settlement. "We have great cause to rejoice this night that our little maid is safe at home," she said.

"I'll make a good search for Brownie to-morrow," declared Captain Enos, "but I fear now that the Indians have her."

The good couple decided that it would be best to say as little of Anne's adventure as possible, and to tell her not to talk of it to her playmates.

"I'll caution the mothers," said Mrs. Stoddard, "but 'tis no use for our little people to frighten themselves by wondering about Indians. Maybe they will not come near us again, and they'll not dare to make another mistake." So but little was made of Anne's escape from the squaws, although the children now stayed at home more closely, and Anne did not often stray far from Aunt Martha.

CHAPTER VII

OUT TO SEA

CAPTAIN ENOS and the boys returned without having found any trace of the missing cattle, and the villagers felt it to be a loss hardly to be borne that three of their six cows should have disappeared. The men went about their fishing even more soberly than before, and the women and children mourned loudly.

Amanda Cary waited at the spring each day for Anne's appearance. Sometimes the two little girls did not speak, and again Amanda would make some effort to win Anne's notice.

"Your father is a soldier," she declared one morning, and when Anne nodded smilingly, Amanda ventured a step nearer. "You may come up to my house and see my white kittens if you want to," she said.

There could be no greater temptation to Anne than this. To have a kitten of her own had been one of her dearest wishes, and to see and play with two white kittens, even Amanda's kittens, was a joy not lightly to be given up. But Anne shook her head, and Amanda, surprised and sulky, went slowly back toward home.

The next morning, as Anne went toward the spring, she met Amanda coming up the hill, carrying a white kitten in her arms.

"I was just going up to your house," said Amanda. "I was bringing up this white kitten to give to you."

"Oh, Amanda!" exclaimed Anne, quite forgetting her old dislike of the little girl, and reaching out eager hands for the kitten which Amanda gave to her.

"My mother said that we could not afford to keep two kittens," Amanda explained, "and I thought right off that I would give one to you."

"Thank you, Amanda," and then Anne's face grew sober, "but maybe my Aunt Martha will not want me to keep it," she said.

"I guess she will," ventured Amanda. "I will go with you and find out, and if she be not pleased I'll find some one to take it."

The two little girls trudged silently along over the sandy path. Anne carried the kitten very carefully, and Amanda watched her companion anxiously.

"If Mistress Stoddard says that you may keep the kitten may I stay and play a little while?" she asked as they came near the Stoddard house.

"Yes," answered Anne, "you may stay anyway, and I will show you my playhouse."

Amanda's thin freckled face brightened. "If she won't let you keep the kitten you may come over to my house every day and play with mine," she said; and almost hoped that Mistress Stoddard would not want the little white cat, for Amanda was anxious for a playmate, and Anne was nearer her age than any of the little girls of the settlement.

Mrs. Stoddard was nearly as much pleased with the kitten as Anne herself, and Amanda was told that she was a good little girl, her past unkindness was forgotten, and the two children, taking the kitten with them, went out to the playhouse under the pines. Amanda was allowed to hold the wooden doll, and they played very happily together until disturbed by a loud noise near the shore, then they ran down the little slope to see what was happening.

"It's Brownie!" exclaimed Anne.

"And our cow and the Starkweathers'," declared Amanda. "Where do you suppose they found them?"

Jimmie Starkweather drove Brownie up to the little barn, and Mrs. Stoddard came running out to welcome the wanderer.

"Where did they come from, Jimmie?" she questioned.

"A Truro man has just driven them over," explained Jimmie; "he found them in his pasture, and thinks the Indians dared not kill them or drive them further."

"It's good fortune to get them back," said Mrs. Stoddard. "Now you will have milk for your white kitten, Anne. Since the English sailors rescued you from the Indians, they've not been about so much."

The kitten was almost forgotten in petting and feeding Brownie, and Amanda looked on wonderingly to see Anne bring in bunches of tender grass for the little brown cow to eat.

"I cannot get near to our cow," she said; "she shakes her horns at me, and sniffs, and I dare not feed her," but she resolved to herself that she would try and make friends with the black and white animal of which she had always been afraid.

"Come again, Amanda," said Anne, when Amanda said that she must go home, and the little visitor started off happily toward home, resolving that she would bring over her white kitten the very next day, and wondering if her own father could not make her a doll such as Anne Nelson had.

"Thee must not forget thy knitting, Anne," cautioned Mrs. Stoddard, as Anne came in from a visit to Brownie, holding the white kitten in her arms; " 'twill not be so many weeks now before the frost will be upon us, and I must see to it that your uncle's stockings are ready, and that you have mittens; so you must do your best to help on the stockings," and Mrs. Stoddard handed the girl the big ball of scarlet yarn and the stocking just begun on the shining steel needles.

"Remember, it is knit one and seam," she said. "You can sit in the open doorway, child, and when you have knit round eight times we will call thy stint finished for the morning. This afternoon we must go for cranberries. We will be needing all we can gather before the frost comes."

Anne put the kitten down on the floor and took the stocking, eyeing the scarlet yarn admiringly. She sat down in the open doorway and began her stint, her mind filled with happy thoughts. To have Amanda speak well of her dear father, to know that Brownie was safe in the barn, to possess a white kitten of her own, and, above all, to be knitting herself a pair of scarlet stockings made Anne feel that the world was a very kind and friendly place. The white kitten looked at the moving ball of yarn curiously, and now and then made little springs toward it, greatly to Anne's amusement, but in a few moments she found that her progress was slow, and the white kitten was sent off the broad step to play by itself on the sandy path.

From time to time Mrs. Stoddard would come to look at Anne's knitting, and to praise the smoothness of the work.

"Your uncle says you are to have stout leather shoes," she said. "Elder Haven tells me that there will be six weeks' school this autumn and it be good news."

"Shall I go to school, Aunt Martha?" questioned Anne, looking up from her knitting.

Mrs. Stoddard nodded, smiling down at the eager little face. "Indeed you will. 'Twill be the best of changes for you. Like as not Elder Haven will teach thee to write."

"I know my letters and can spell small words," said Anne.

"I'll teach thee to read if time allows," answered Mrs. Stoddard. "Your Uncle Enos has a fine book of large print; 'Pilgrim's Progress' it's named, and 'tis of interest. We will begin on it for a lesson."

That afternoon found Anne and Mrs. Stoddard busily picking cranberries on the bog beyond the maple grove. Jimmie Starkweather and Amos Cary were also picking there, and before the afternoon finished, Amanda appeared. She came near Anne to pick and soon asked if Anne was to go to Elder Haven's school.

"Yes, indeed," answered Anne, "and maybe I shall be taught writing, and then I can send a letter, if chance offers, to my father."

"You are always talking and thinking about your father," responded Amanda; "if he should want you to leave the Stoddards I suppose you would go in a minute."

Anne's face grew thoughtful. Never had she been so happy and well cared for as at the Stoddards'; to go to her father would perhaps mean that she would go hungry and half-clad as in the old days, but she remembered her father's loneliness, how he had always tried to do all that he could for her, and she replied slowly, "I guess my father might need me more than Aunt Martha and Uncle Enos. They have each other, and my father has only me."

Amanda asked no more questions, but she kept very close to Anne and watched her with a new interest.

"I wish I could read," she said, as, their baskets well filled, the two girls walked toward home. "I don't even know my letters."

"I can teach you those," said Anne eagerly. "I can teach you just as my dear father did me. We used to go out on the beach in front of our house and he would mark out the letters in the sand and tell me their names, and then I would mark them out. Sometimes we would make letters as long as I am tall. Would you like me to teach you?"

"Yes, indeed. Let's go down to the shore now," urged Amanda.

"We'd best leave our berries safely at home," replied Anne, who did not forget her adventure with the Indian squaws, and was now very careful not to go too far from the settlement, and so it was decided that they should hurry home and leave their baskets and meet on the smooth sandy beach near Anne's old home.

Anne was the first to reach the place. She brought with her two long smooth sticks and had already traced out an enormous A when Amanda appeared.

"This is 'A,'" she called out. "'A' is for Anne, and for Amanda."

"I know I can remember that," said Amanda, "and I can make it, too."

It was not long before a long row of huge letters were shaped along the beach, and when Amos came down he looked at them wonderingly.

"Amos, can you spell my name?" asked his sister.

"Of course I can!" replied the boy scornfully. "I'll mark it out for you," and in a short time Amanda was repeating over and over again the letters which formed her name.

After Amos had marked out his sister's name in the sand he started along the shore to where a dory lay, just floating on the swell of the incoming tide.

"Amos is going to fish for flounders," said Amanda; "he catches a fine mess almost every afternoon for mother to cook for supper. He's a great help."

"Want to fish?" called out Amos as the two little girls came near the boat and watched him bait his hooks with clams which he had dug and brought with him.

"Oh, yes," said Anne; "do you think I could catch enough for Uncle Enos's supper?"

"Yes, if you'll hurry," answered the boy; "climb in over the bow."

The barefooted children splashed through the shallow curl of the waves on the beach, and clambered over the high bow of the dory. Amos baited their lines, and with a word of advice as to the best place to sit, he again turned to his own fishing and soon pulled in a big, flopping, resisting flounder.

"The tide isn't right," he declared after a few minutes when no bite came to take the bait. "I'm going to cast off and pull a little way down shore over the flats. They'll be sure to bite there. You girls sit still. You can troll your lines if you want to. You may catch something."

So Anne and Amanda sat very still while Amos sprang ashore, untied the rope from the stout post sunk in the beach, pushed the boat into deeper water, and jumped in as it floated clear from the shore.

It was a big, clumsy boat, and the oars were heavy; but Amos was a stout boy of twelve used to boats and he handled the oars very skilfully.

"The tide's just turning," he said; " 'twill take us down shore without much rowing."

"But 'twill be hard coming back," suggested Amanda.

"Pooh! Hard! I guess I could row through any water in this harbor," bragged Amos, bending to his oar so lustily that he broke one of the wooden thole-pins, unshipped his oar, and went over backward into the bottom of the boat, losing his hold on the oar as he fell. He scrambled quickly back to his seat, and endeavored to swing the dory about with one oar so that he could reach the one now floating rapidly away. But he could not get within reach of it.

"You girls move forward," he commanded; "I'll have to scull," and moving cautiously to the stern of the boat he put his remaining oar in the notch cut for it and began to move it regularly back and forth.

"Are you going inshore, Amos?" questioned his sister.

"What for?" asked the boy. "I've got one good oar, haven't I? We can go along first-rate."

"It's too bad to lose a good oar," said Amanda.

"Father won't care," said Amos reassuringly; " 'twa'n't a good oar. The blade was split; 'twas liable to harm somebody. He'll not worry at losing it."

The dory went along very smoothly under Amos's sculling and with the aid of the tide. Amanda and Anne, their lines trailing overboard, watched eagerly for a bite, and before long Anne had pulled in a good-sized plaice, much to Amos's satisfaction. He drew in his oar to help her take out the hook, and had just completed this task when Amanda called out:

"Amos! Amos! the oar's slipping!"

The boy turned quickly and grabbed at the vanishing oar, but he was too late—it had slid into the water. They were now some distance from shore and the tide was setting strongly toward the mouth of the harbor. Amos looked after the oar and both of the little girls looked at Amos.

"What are we going to do now?" asked Amanda. "We can't ever get back to shore."

CHAPTER VIII

ON THE ISLAND

Amos made no answer to his sister's frightened exclamation. He was well used to the harbor, as he often went fishing with his father, and had been on cruises of several days. Tide and wind both took the boat swiftly toward Long Point, a low, narrow sand-beach, which ran out into the harbor.

"We'll run straight into Long Point if the wind don't change," said Amos.

Anne had held fast to her line and now felt it tugging strongly in her grasp.

"I've caught something!" she exclaimed, "and I don't believe I can ever pull it in."

Amos reached across and seized the line. "Gee!" he exclaimed, "I'll bet it's a cod," and he pulled valiantly. It took all the boy's strength to get the big fish into the boat. I'll bet it weighs ten pounds," declared Amos proudly, quite forgetting in his pleasure over the big fish that the boat was still moving swiftly away from the settlement.

"Amos, Amos, just see how fast we are going," said Amanda; "we'll be carried right out to sea."

"Well, then some vessel will pick us up and bring us back," answered her brother, "but it looks now as if we would bring up on Long Point, and we can walk home from there easy enough. It's only a couple of miles."

"Perhaps we could get home before they missed us," suggested Anne, hopefully.

Amos nodded; he was still busy with the big fish, but in a few moments he began to look anxiously ahead.

"The wind's pulling round to the southeast," he said. "I guess we sha'n't hit Long Point after all."

"We're going right into Wood End," declared Amanda, "or else to House Point Island. Oh, Amos, if we land on that island nobody will ever find us."

"It will be better to land anywhere than to be carried beyond Race Point," said Amos; "the wind is growing stronger every minute."

The three children no longer felt any interest in their fish-lines. Amos had drawn his line in when they started off from shore, and Amanda had let go of hers when the first oar was lost. Anne was the only one who had kept a firm hold on her line, and now she drew it in and coiled it carefully around the smooth piece of wood to which it was fastened.

"I'll get this boat ashore some way," declared Amos boldly; "if we run near any land I'll jump overboard with the painter and pull the dory to shore. I'll get up in the bow now so's to be ready."

Neither of the little girls said anything. Amanda was ready to cry with fear, and Anne was watching the sky anxiously.

"The sun is all covered up with clouds," she said, and before Amos could answer there came a patter of raindrops. The wind, too, increased in force and the waves grew higher. Anne and Amanda crouched low in the boat, while Amos in the bow peered anxiously ahead.

Within the curve of the shore of Race Point lay House Point Island, where Amos hoped they might land. It was a small island partly covered with scrubby thickets but no tall trees, and with shallow water all about it. Amos was sure that he could pull the clumsy boat to shore if the wind would only set a little in that direction. The September afternoon was growing late, the sky was now completely overcast, and the rain falling steadily.

"We're getting near the island," said Amos. "I'll slide overboard in a minute, and all you girls need do is keep still till I tell you to jump," and Amos, the painter of the dory in one hand, slipped over the high bow of the boat and struck out for shore. He was a strong swimmer, and managed to change the course of the boat so that it swung in toward the shallow water, and in a few minutes Amos got a foothold on the sand, and pulled strongly on the rope until the boat was well out of the outward sweep of the current.

"Now jump out," he commanded; "you on one side, Anne, and Amanda on the other, and take hold of the side and help pull the boat ashore."

The two girls obeyed instantly, and the three dripping children struggled up the beach, pulling the dory beyond reach of the tide.

"We must be sure this boat is safe," said Amos; "if we can get it up a little further, we can tip it up on one side and crawl under and get out of the rain."

The codfish, plaice and flounder Amos took out carefully and carried to a large rock further up the beach. "We'll have to eat those fish if we stay here very long," he said.

It grew dark early and the children, under the shelter of the boat, peered out at the rushing waves, listened to the wind, and were very glad that they were on shore, even if it was an island and miles away from home.

"Nobody can find us to-night," said Anne, "but prob'ly to-morrow morning, first thing, my Uncle Enos and your father will take a boat and come sailing right down after us."

"How will they know where we are?" whimpered Amanda. "We'll have to stay here always; I know we shall."

"If we do I'll build a brush house," said Amos hopefully, "and there's lots of beach-plums grow on this island, I've heard folks say; and we'll cook those fish and I'll bet I can find mussels along the shore."

"We can't cook anything," said Anne, "for we can't make any fire."

"I can make a fire when things get dry," said Amos; "how do you suppose Indians make fires when they are off like this? An Indian doesn't care where he is because he knows how to get things to eat and how to cook them, and how to make a shelter. I've wished lots of times that I'd had the chances to learn things that Indians have."

The boat proved a shelter against the wind, and the long night wore slowly away. Amos slept soundly, but neither Anne nor Amanda could sleep, except in short naps from which they quickly awakened. The storm ceased in the night and the sun came up and sent its warm beams down on the shivering children, who crept out from the dory and ran and jumped about on the sand until they were quite warm and very hungry.

Amos went searching along the shore for the round dark-shelled mussels which he knew were good to eat, and Anne and Amanda went up toward the thick-growing bushes beyond the sand-banks to look for beach-plums.

"Look, Anne! Look! Did you ever see so many on one bush?" exclaimed Amanda, and the bush was indeed well filled with the appetizing fruit.

"We must take a lot to Amos," said Anne, "for he is getting mussels for us now."

"Yes, indeed," agreed Amanda; "do you suppose they will come after us this morning, Anne?"

"Of course they will, first thing," replied Anne hopefully, so that Amanda grew more cheerful, and when they got back to the boat with aprons full of beachplums and found Amos waiting for them with a fine lot of fresh mussels they quite forgot to be troubled or unhappy. The sun was shining brightly, the blue water looked calm and smooth, and the wind had entirely gone. They ate the plums and mussels hungrily.

"We'd better look around a little," said Amos, when they had finished, "and see if we can find a good place for a brush house. We ought to build it near the shore so that we can keep a watch for any passing boat."

"Won't father find us to-day?" asked Amanda anxiously.

"Can't tell," replied her brother; "anyway we want to get ready to build a house, for we might have to stay here a week."

"I believe you want to stay a week, Amos Cary!" exclaimed his sister.

"I'd just as soon stay as not," said Amos, "if I can find some rotten wood like the Indians use to start a fire; but it isn't much use to look for it until things begin to dry up."

Amos, followed closely by the little girls, went up the bank and toward a place where grew a thicket of small pines. "We can break off a lot of these branches and carry them down to the shore," he said, "and fix some beds of them under one side of the dory. It will be better than sleeping on the sand."

They made several trips back and forth to the boat with armfuls of pine boughs until they each had quite a pile, long and wide enough for a bed, and high enough to keep them well off the sand. But Amos was not satisfied.

"This sand-bank makes a good back for a house," he said; "now if we could only build up sides, and fix some kind of a roof, it would make a fine house."

"Won't the dory do for one side?" asked Anne.

"No," said Amos, "but we can pile up heaps of sand here on each side of our beds, right against this sand-bank, and that will make three sides of a house, and then we'll think of something for the roof."

So they all went to work piling up the sand. It was hard work, and it took a long time before the loose sand could be piled up high enough for Anne and Amanda to crouch down behind.

"I'm dreadful hungry," said Amanda, after they had worked steadily for some time; "let's rest and eat some mussels and beach-plums," and Amos and Anne were both quite ready to stop work.

"It must be past noon now," said Amos, looking at the sun, "and there hasn't a boat come in sight."

Anne had begun to look very serious. "My Aunt Martha may think that I have run away," she said, as they sat leaning back against the piles of warm sand.

"No, she won't" Amos assured her, "for they'll find out right off that Amanda and I are gone, and father's dory, and it won't take father or Captain Enos long to guess what's happened; only they'll think that we have been carried out to sea."

The little girls were very silent after this, until Amos jumped up saying: "I've just thought of a splendid plan. We'll pile up sand just as high as we can on both sides. Then I'll take those fish-lines and cut them in pieces long enough to reach across from one sand heap to the other, and tie rocks on each end of the lines and put them across."

"I don't think fish-lines will make much of a roof," said Amanda.

"And after I get the lines across," went on Amos, not heeding what his sister had said, "we'll lay these pine boughs across the lines. See? We can have the branches come well over each side and lap one row over another and make a fine roof," and Amos jumped about, greatly pleased with his own invention.

They all returned to piling up sand and before sunset had made walls taller than their heads, and Amos had put the lines across and the covering of pine boughs, so that it was nicely roofed in.

"It will be a lot better than sleeping under the dory," said Anne, as they looked proudly at the little shelter, "and there's pine boughs enough left for beds, too!"

"We can get more to-morrow," said Amos, "and we'll have a fire to-morrow if I can only find some punk, and cook those fish."

"But I want to go home to-morrow," said Amanda; "I know my mother wants me. We've got a boat; can't you make an oar and row us home, Amos?"

"There isn't anything to make an oar out of," answered Amos.

They made their supper on more mussels and beach-plums, and then lay down on their beds of boughs in the little enclosure. They could see the moon shining over the water, the big dory hauled up in front of their shelter, and they all felt very glad that they were not drifting out at sea.

Amos had many plans in his head, and was eager for another day to come that he might carry them out, but Amanda and Anne went to sleep hoping only that the next day would see one of the big fishing-boats of Provincetown come sailing up to the island to take them safely home.

CHAPTER IX

THE CASTAWAYS

"My, it was cold last night," shivered Amanda, as she and Anne went toward the spring of fresh water which bubbled up near the shore for their morning drink. "I do wish Amos would plan some way to get us home to-day."

"How can he?" asked Anne; "he hasn't any oars, and see what a long way it is across the water to Long Point. He couldn't swim that far."

"Yes, he could, too," declared Amanda, "and when the tide is out the water is so shallow that you can see the yellow sand shining through. He could swim some and walk some, and he'd get over there all right; then he could walk home and tell father and Captain Enos and they would come right after us."

"Why doesn't he go then?" questioned Anne. "I do know that my Aunt Martha is sadly worried; it is full two days since we set forth."

"Amos likes to stay here," said Amanda, lowering her voice to a whisper; "he thinks it is fun to live as Indians do, and he doesn't want to go home. If he gets enough to eat he'll stay and stay, and then he can tell Jimmie Starkweather of being wrecked on an island."

"Couldn't we get across to Long Point?" asked Anne.

"No. We can't swim, and 'twould be foolish to try," answered Amanda.

"We'll have cooked fish for dinner," said Amos as they ate beach-plums for breakfast. "I'm sure I can find some punk somewhere on this island, and while I am looking for it you girls gather all the dry twigs you can find, make a good-sized hole in the sand and fill it up with dry stuff that will take fire quickly, and I'll show you how Indians cook."

"I'd rather have some Indian meal mush," replied Amanda; "can't you swim across to Long Point, Amos, and hurry home and send some one after us?"

Amos looked at her in astonishment, and then smiled broadly. "I know a better way than that," he said, and without waiting to answer the girl's eager questions he ran off toward the thicket of pines.

"We'll dig the hole in the sand, and then find some dry wood," said Anne; "anything cooked will taste good, won't it?"

"Amos knows some way to get us home," said Amanda, "and he's got to tell us what it is, and start just as soon as he cooks his old fish. I wonder what it is!"

Now that Amanda saw a prospect of getting home she felt more cheerful and so did Anne; and they gathered dry brush, bits of bark and handfuls of the sunburned beach-grass until the hole in the sand was filled, and there was a good-sized heap of dry brush over it.

"Do you suppose Amos can really make a fire?" asked Anne.

"I guess he can," said Amanda. "Amos is real smart at queer things like that, that other boys don't think about."

"I've found some!" shouted Amos, as he leaped down the bank; "just a little bit, in the stump of an old oak tree up here. Now wait till I get the thole-pins, and you'll see," and he ran toward the dory and returned with a pair of smooth, round thole-pins, and sat down on the sand in front of the brush heap. The precious piece of punk was carefully wrapped in a piece of the sleeve of his flannel blouse.

"I had to tear it off," he explained, when Amanda pointed to the ragged slit, "for punk must be kept dry or it isn't a bit of use."

He now spread the bit of flannel on the sand in front of him, and kneeling down beside it began to rub the thole-pins across each other as fast as he could move his hands. Anne and Amanda, kneeling on each side of him, looked on with anxious eyes.

"There's a spark!" at last shouted Amanda.

The spark fell on the dry punk, in an instant the punk caught and there were several sparks, then Amos held a wisp of dry grass in front of it and blew vigorously, and the smouldering punk flamed up, the grass caught, Amos thrust it under the dry brush, and in less than a minute the whole mass was burning briskly. The children all jumped about it in delight.

"My, I wish we could have had a fire like that last night, when I was so cold," said Amanda.

"We'll keep it burning now," said Amos. "I've always wanted to start a fire this way. I think it's better than flint and tinder," for in those days the wooden splint matches were not known in the settlement, and fires were started by rubbing flint and steel together until a spark caught.

"We are going home this afternoon," said Amanda, so firmly that Amos looked at her in surprise.

"What for?" he asked. "I think it's fine here. We've got a house and a fire, and we'll have fish enough to last—"

"We are going home," interrupted Amanda; "it's horrid here, and everybody will be afraid we are drowned."

A little smile crept over Amos's freckled face.

" 'Twill indeed be a tale to tell Jimmie Stark-weather," he said, looking admiringly at the brush-covered shelter, and then at the brisk fire. " 'Tis a ship-wreck such as no boy on the settlement has had."

Amos asked no more questions, but sent the girls after more dry brush, while he dug another hole in the sand. Then with a long stick he pushed the hot wood and coals from the first hole into the second, and carefully laid the big plaice fish on the hot sand, pushed a thick covering of hot sand over it, and started a new fire on top of it.

" 'Twill be baked to a turn," he said to his sister and Anne; " 'tis the way the Indians cook fish and mussels and clams. I have seen them."

"We'll go home as soon as we can eat it," said Amanda; " 'twill be low tide by that time, and if you have no better plan for us, Amos, Anne and I will wade to Long Point."

"Wade!" repeated Amos scornfully; "you'd be drowned!"

"Then tell us your plan," urged Amanda, while Anne looked at him pleadingly. She had thought much about her father as she lay awake under the roof of pine boughs, and wondered if some word from him might not have reached the settlement. She thought, too, about the scarlet stockings, and wished herself back in the little brown house on the hill. So she said, "We must go home, Amos."

"I wish you girls had stayed home," muttered Amos; "if some of the boys had come we'd have had a good time here; but girls always want to go home. Well, I'll get you to Long Point without swimming," and again Amos smiled, for he had a secret of his own that he knew would greatly surprise Amanda and Anne.

It was not long before he began scraping the hot embers from the sand under which the fish was cooking. Then he poked the hot sand away, and there lay the plaice, steaming and smoking, and sending out an appetizing odor.

"There!" said Amos proudly, as he managed to cut off a piece with his jack-knife for each of the girls, "that's as good fish as you ever tasted."

"It's the best," said Anne, and Amanda ate hungrily. Indeed the children were all so hungry that they devoured the entire fish.

"If you'll stay till to-morrow I'll cook the cod," said Amos, but both Amanda and Anne said they wanted to go home. So Amos with their help pushed and dragged the dory into the water, and then telling the girls to stay right by the boat until he returned, started off up the beach to where he had found the mussels. In a few minutes they saw him running back.

"Look, Amanda!" exclaimed Anne, "he's found an oar!"

The little girls could hardly believe it possible; but Amos was smiling and seemed to think it was a great joke.

"I found it yesterday morning, the very first thing, when you were off after beach-plums," he explained, "and I hid it, because I knew if I told you I'd found an oar you'd want to start for home right off; and as long as we were here I wanted some fun out of it. Now jump in, and I'll scull you over to Long Point in no time."

The girls were too glad at the idea of really starting for home to blame Amos for keeping them on the island so long, but Anne thought to herself that she was sure that none of the Starkweather boys would have hidden the oar. "Amos is smart, but he's selfish," she decided, as the boy bent to the big oar and sent the clumsy boat toward Long Point.

" 'Tis a good oar, better than the one I lost," said Amos, "and I do think 'twas lost from one of the English ships. There's a big 'S' burned into the handle. Mayhap it belonged to the 'Somerset.' If so I'm glad they lost it."

" 'Twas the 'Somerset' ran down my father's boat and nigh drowned him," said Anne, "and the sailors lent him no help, but laughed to see him struggle till he reached near enough their ship to clamber up."

"I wish I could be a soldier like your father," said Amos, and at this Anne looked upon him more kindly.

"Scull faster, Amos," urged Amanda; "the sun is not two hours high, and 'tis a long walk through the sand before we can get home. I do hope we'll get there before milking time that I may have a drink of warm milk."

When the boat touched the sandy shore of Long Point, Anne and Amanda scrambled over the bow and urged Amos to hurry.

"I must make the boat safe," he said; " 'twould be a sad loss to have the tide take her out. And I'll hide this good oar, too. To-morrow Jimmie Starkweather and I will sail down and tow her back, and maybe take a look at the island," and Amos looked back regretfully to the shores they had just left.

The dory was drawn up beyond reach of the tide, the oar hidden under the sand, and the children started on their walk toward home. The distance was but two miles, but walking through the loose sand was hard and tiresome.

"I slip back a step every step I take," said Anne; "look, the sun is nearly out of sight now."

"The milk will be strained and set ere this," said Amanda mournfully; "there's not even a beach-plum grows on this point, and the long grass cuts my feet whenever I come near it."

"You could have had another baked fish by this time if you would have stayed on the island," said Amos complainingly.

After this the children plodded on in silence for a long time. The harvest moon rose beyond the harbor and smiled down upon them. There was a silvery glint all over the water, and as they came round one of the big piles of sand, which are so often seen along the coast of Cape Cod, they all stopped and looked out across the harbor. It was Amos who pointed toward a big ship riding at anchor, perhaps a mile from the shore.

"There's the 'Somerset' back again," he said. "I wonder if there's any harm done at the settlement?"

CHAPTER X

SAFE AT HOME

It was late in the evening when the three tired, hungry children reached the settlement. Amanda and Amos ran up the path to their door and Anne plodded on toward Mrs. Stoddard's, nearly a half mile from the Cary house.

There was not a light to be seen in the village, but Anne could see the shining lanterns on the "Somerset" sending narrow rays of light across the water. But she was too tired to think of the British ship, or of anything except how good it would be to sleep in a real bed again.

At Mrs. Stoddard's door she stood for a moment wondering if she could not creeep in and up-stairs without waking Uncle Enos and Aunt Martha; she tried the door softly, but it was bolted, so she rattled the latch and called, "Aunt Martha! Uncle Enos!" a sudden fear filling her heart that they might not hear her and that she might have to sleep on the door-step.

But in an instant she heard steps hurrying across the kitchen floor, the big bolt was pulled back, the door swung open, and Anne was warmly clasped in

Aunt Martha's arms. Uncle Enos hurried close behind her, and Anne was drawn into the kitchen with many exclamations of wonder and joy.

"Light a candle that we may look at her," said Aunt Martha, "and start up a fire. 'Tis a chilly night, and the child must have some warm porridge."

It was not long before the fire was burning brightly, a kettle of hot water bubbling cheerfully, that Anne might have a warm bath to rest and soothe her tired limbs, and Anne, sitting on Aunt Martha's lap, was eating a bowl of hot porridge and telling the story of her adventures.

"House Point Island, eh?" said Uncle Enos; " 'tis lucky there was an island just there, even so low a one as that. In a hundred years or so the tides and waves will sweep it away."

Anne told of the brush-covered shelter, of Amos making a fire and cooking the fish, and of their journey home, while her kind friends listened eagerly.

"We feared the boat had been carried out to sea and that our little maid was lost," said Aunt Martha, "and the men have looked for you all about the shore. The 'Somerset' is in harbor and its crew are doing much mischief on shore, so that we have had much to disturb us. What a tangle of hair this is for me to brush out," she added, passing a tender hand over Anne's dark locks.

How good the warm water felt to Anne's bruised feet; and she was sure that nothing ever tasted so good as the porridge. The rough hair was brushed into smooth braids, and it was a very happy little girl who went to sleep in the upper chamber with her wooden doll beside her, and the white kitten curled up on the foot of her bed.

"I'm glad I'm not a little Indian girl," was Anne's last thought before she went to sleep.

It was late the next morning when she awoke. Her soiled and torn clothes were not to be seen, but a dress of clean cotton and a fresh pinafore lay on the wooden stool.

"My, it's nice to be clean," thought Anne, remembering the uncomfortable efforts that she and Amanda had made to wash their faces in water from the island spring.

"It's near noon, dear child," said Mrs. Stoddard, as Anne came into the kitchen. "You shall have a boiled egg for your breakfast, and I am cooking a fine johnnycake for you before the fire. You must be nigh starved. To think of that Amos Cary hiding the oar instead of fetching you straight home."

"But he worked all the time to make a house for us, and to cook the fish," explained Anne, "and he speaks well of my father. I like him better than when he called me names."

"Of course you do, child; and I did not think him so smart a boy as he proves. 'Twas no small thing to start a fire as he did."

" 'Twas Amanda made him come home," said Anne'; "she told him we would walk through the water to the Point, and then he said he would fetch us."

"Your Encle Enos thinks Amos may make a good sailor," said Aunt Martha. "Indeed, if it were not for these British ships hovering about our shores it is likely that Skipper Cary would have been off to the Banks and taken Amos with him."

The "Banks" were the fishing grounds off the island of Newfoundland, and for several years the Cape Cod fishermen had made summer cruises there, coming home with big cargoes of fine fish which they sold in the Boston market at excellent prices. These fishing grounds were call the "Banks," because of the heavy banks of fog which settled down in that region.

After Anne had finished her breakfast she went to Mrs. Stoddard's big work-basket, and took out her knitting-work.

"May I not knit a long time to-day, Aunt Martha?" she asked. "My feet ache sorely, and I should like well to knit."

"That is right," answered Mrs. Stoddard, nodding her approval. "Your Uncle Enos drove Brownie over

SHE WORKED STEADILY

the hill where the sailors from the 'Somerset' will not be like to see her, and we will both stay indoors to-day and knit. Maybe we shall begin to read to-day, also."

"After I have knit a good stint," said Anne, "for 'twill be time for stockings soon."

It was a happy morning for the little girl. She worked steadily and carefully until Captain Enos came up from the shore for his noon meal.

"Well, well," he said smilingly, "now this seems good—to see our little maid safe at home by the window with her knitting. I saw Mistress Starkweather as I came home, and she bade me tell you she should walk this way to see you this afternoon. 'Tis a great day for Amos," continued the captain; "he tells all the boys in the village of his great adventure in rounding Long Point and living two days on an island. You'd think he seen Terra del Fuego, to say the least."

"And what is Terra del Fuego?" asked Anne wonderingly.

" 'Tis a far island, Anne, in warm southern seas, such a distance as few Cape Cod sailors ever go; though we go to most places, I will say," he added with a hearty laugh.

"Amos and Jimmie Starkweather were all for sailing off this morning to bring the dory home," he continued, "but a boatload of the 'Somerset's' men stopped them and sent them ashore, threatening to dismast any sloop that put up a sail in this harbor without their permission."

Anne knit steadily on, thinking of her father, and wondering if these men on board the "Somerset" had any knowledge of him. But she asked no questions, knowing that Captain Enos would tell her if any news came.

The scarlet stockings had made good progress when Mistress Starkweather was seen coming up the sandy path. Anne ran to the door to meet her, and the good woman kissed her heartily. "To think of the danger you were in, dear child," she said, as Anne led her into the sunny kitchen and drew out the most comfortable chair for her.

"Amos was not afraid," said Anne, "but Amanda and I did wish ourselves home."

"I'll warrant that boy would not be afraid of the water, storm, or no storm," said Mrs. Stoddard, drawing her own chair near to her neighbor's; "yet Captain Enos tells that he fled from our Anne here when she threw water at him," and the two women smiled, remembering the little girl's loyal defense of her absent father.

"School is to begin next Monday, if all goes well," continued Mrs. Starkweather, "and beside that the minister declared we must all come more punctually to church. Last Sunday there were but seven in the meeting-house," and Mrs. Starkweather's face grew sober.

"I shall not have time to learn to read long words before Monday," said Anne anxiously.

"I planned to teach the child a little before school begins," explained Mrs. Stoddard, "from Captain Enos's 'Pilgrim's Progress.' His mother bought the book in Boston, and he treasures it."

"And no wonder," replied Mrs. Starkweather; "beside the Bible there are few books in any household in the settlement. I doubt if the minister can lay claim to a half dozen. He has his knowledge in his head."

"And so should all people have," said Mrs. Stoddard. "Anne, go to the big red chest in my bedroom and take out the book that lies there and fetch it to me. Mayhap Mistress Starkweather would like to see it."

Anne quickly obeyed. The big red chest was one that Captain Enos had carried when he went on whaling voyages. It had handles of twisted rope, and a huge padlock swung from an iron loop in front. Anne lifted the top and reached in after the book; but the chest was deep; there were only a few articles on the bottom of the chest, and she could not reach it. So she pushed the lid back until it rested against the wall, and stepped into the chest, stooping down to pick up the book As she leaned over, bang,—down came the lid to the chest, shutting Anne closely in. For an instant the child was too frightened to move, as she lay on her face in the big chest; then she tried to sit up, and found she could not. She tried to call "Aunt Martha," but her voice sounded thick and muffled.

In the kitchen the two neighbors sat waiting for Anne and the book.

"Anne! Anne!" called Mrs. Stoddard. "Why, the child is usually so spry. I wonder what keeps her," and she went into the bedroom.

"Did Anne slip out while we talked?" she called back to Mrs. Starkweather. "She's not here."

Just then there came a sound from the chest. "Pity's sake!" exclaimed Mrs. Stoddard. "I do believe Anne is in the chest," and she hastened to swing back the big lid and to lift the half-stifled child out.

"Did you ever!" she said. "How came you in the chest, child?"

"I got in to get the book and the lid fell on me," half whispered Anne, clinging to Mrs. Stoddard's skirts.

"Well, well, child, there is no harm done," said Mrs. Stoddard, "but 'tis not a safe thing to get into chests. I will get the book. I thought your arms were longer," and Mrs. Stoddard reached into the sea-chest and drew out a long black-covered book. "It has many pictures," she said. "I wonder I have not shown it to Anne before."

Mrs. Starkweather looked at the book admiringly, and Mrs. Stoddard took Anne in her lap that they might all enjoy the pictures together.

"Look," she said; "here is Christian setting forth on his journey, and here are Obstinate and Pliable, two of his neighbors, following him to urge him to come home."

Anne looked at the picture eagerly. She had never seen pictures in a book before, and it seemed very wonderful to her.

"It is a good story," said Mrs. Starkweather. "True, it is said to be but a dream, but I read it in my youth and liked it well. It has been a treat to see it, Mrs. Stoddard. 'Tis seldom I have so care-free an after-noon. Six boys to look after keep me busy," and the good woman rose from her chair and with cordial words of good-bye started for home.

"I wish I could read this book," said Anne, turning the leaves over carefully and wondering what the pic-tures meant.

"So you shall. We'll read a little now. Come, you shall spell out the words, and I will speak them for you and tell you their meaning."

An hour later when Captain Enos stepped into the kitchen he declared that he thought school had begun there; and while Mrs. Stoddard hurried about to prepare supper Uncle Enos continued Anne's reading lesson.

"Perhaps I can read this book after I go to school," said Anne.

"That you can," answered the captain.

"And I will learn to write," said Anne, "and it may be I could send a letter to my dear father."

"That is a good child," said Captain Enos, patting the dark head; "learn to write and we'll set about starting the letter to your father as soon as you have it ready."

"I shall have much to tell him," said Anne, smiling up into Uncle Enos's kind face.

"And he'll have a good deal to tell you," replied Captain Enos. "I wish I could see him myself. I'd like news of what's going on in Boston."

CHAPTER XI

THE playhouse under the pines was almost forgotten as the days grew colder, and the fall rains came, with high winds; and Anne's scarlet stocking was now long enough for Aunt Martha to "set the heel" and begin to shape the foot. School had begun in Elder Haven's sitting-room, with fourteen scholars, and Anne was learning to write.

"Master Haven says I write my own name nicely," she said at the end of the first week, "and that by the time school closes he thinks I can write a letter."

Captain Enos nodded approvingly. He and Anne were sitting before a bright fire of driftwood in the pleasant kitchen, while Mrs. Stoddard had gone to Mrs. Starkweather's for more scarlet yarn. Anne was knitting busily; her wooden doll sat on the floor, and the white kitten was curled up close to the little girl's feet. Captain Enos had several pieces of smooth cedar wood on a stool near his chair, and was at work upon one with his sharp jack-knife.

"Well, well!" he said, looking up from his whittling. "That will please thy father, Anne. And learn as fast as you can, for I see a fair chance of sending a letter to Boston, when one is ready; and then thy father could soon get it."

"Oh, Uncle Enos!" exclaimed Anne, "if there be a chance to send a letter could you not write for me? It may be when I can write there will be no chance to send a letter."

Captain Enos nodded. "You are a wise child," he said. "My writing isn't the plainest in the world, but I'll do my best. I have some sheets of good smooth paper in my sea-chest, and a good quill pen, too. Elder Haven fixed the pen for me from the feather of a wild goose I killed on the marshes last spring. But I do not think there is such a thing as ink in the house; but I can make a fair ink with the juice of the elderberry and a fair lot of soot from the chimney. So think up what you wish to tell your father, Anne, and if it storms to-morrow we'll write the letter."

"How will you send it, Uncle Enos?" asked Anne, forgetting to knit and turning eager eyes toward the captain.

"Sshh!" said Captain Enos. " 'Tis a secret—hardly to be whispered. But there is a good-hearted sailor-man on board the British ship. We have had some talk together on the shore, and he told me that he liked thy father; and that he did not blame him for escaping from the ship."

Anne nodded smilingly, and reached down and picked up her wooden doll.

"Has the sailorman any little girl?" she asked.

"That he has," said Captain Enos. "He told me that he had two small maids of his own in Plymouth, England, far across the ocean; and he asked if I knew aught of John Nelson's little girl."

"That's me!" said Anne, holding the wooden doll tight.

"Yes," said Captain Enos, "and he said that he might find a chance to send some word to thy father that you were a good and happy child. Then I told him, Anne, that you planned to write a letter, and he said he'd take it to Boston, and then 'twould soon reach thy father."

"I wish I could hear the sailorman speak of my father," said Anne, "and tell me of his little girls in England."

"Mayhap you can, child. He comes ashore after water each day. A stout man he is, with reddish hair and good honest blue eyes. He tells me his name is William Trull. If you see such a man you may speak to him."

"Uncle Enos! That is the sailorman who saved me from the Indian women, and brought me safe home," exclaimed Anne. "Do you not remember?"

"Indeed I do, Anne. And I thought the name would mean something to you," replied Captain Enos.

Anne smiled happily. It was good news to hear from the sailorman, and to know that he was a friend of her father's.

"What are you making, Uncle Enos?" asked Anne, as the captain put down one smooth bit of wood and picked up another.

Captain Enos pointed to Anne's wooden doll and whispered, "I'm afraid Martha Stoddard Nelson will hear. Put her down behind your chair and come over here, and I'll tell you."

Anne set the doll down carefully, with its head turned away from Captain Enos, and tiptoed across the little space between them.

"I'm making a chair for Martha Stoddard Nelson," whispered Captain Enos, "for a surprise. And you mustn't tell her a word about it till it is all ready for her to sit in."

Anne laughed. To have a secret with Uncle Enos was about the most delightful thing she could imagine; and to have it mean a fine cedar chair for her doll to sit in was the best kind of a secret.

"You mustn't let Martha Stoddard Nelson face toward me more than you can help," went on Uncle Enos. "You don't think she has noticed what I am doing, do you?"

"No," whispered Anne. "I'll be very careful, and let her stay up-stairs a good deal until the chair is finished."

"That will be a good plan," said Uncle Enos, "and there comes your Aunt Martha. I hear her at the door."

Anne ran to open the door and Mrs. Stoddard came in smiling and rosy from her walk in the sharp wind. The white kitten jumped up and came running toward her, and the good woman looked about the cheerful room as if she thought it the finest place in the world.

"I have more scarlet yarn," she said, sitting down near Captain Enos, "and I have a present for thee, Anne; something that Mistress Starkweather sent thee with her love," and Mrs. Stoddard handed Anne a small package.

"It's a box!" declared the little girl, taking off the paper in which it was wrapped, "and see how sweet it smells."

" 'Tis of sandalwood," said Captain Enos. "There must be many such in the settlement, for 'twas but a few years ago that some of our men came back from a voyage to Ceylon, and fetched such boxes in their chests."

"Open it, Anne," said Mrs. Stoddard, and Anne carefully took off the cover.

"Look, look!" she exclaimed, holding out the box toward Aunt Martha; "what are these shining things;

all pink and round?" and she picked up a string of pink coral beads and held them up.

"Coral beads!" said Aunt Martha. "Mistress Starkweather said that she thought when her husband brought them home she would keep them for a little girl of her own; but since she has but six boys, she says she knows of no little girl to whom she would rather give them than to thee, Anne. And you must go down to-morrow before school begins and thank her properly."

"Coral beads!" repeated Anne, holding up the pink beads and touching them softly. "May I put them around my neck, Aunt Martha?"

"Indeed you may, child. See, here is a clasp of bright gold to hold them," and Mrs. Stoddard fastened the beads around Anne's neck.

" 'Tis a fine gift," said Captain Enos admiringly, "and shows a kind heart in Mistress Starkweather."

"I wish my father could see," said Anne. "When he knows about my scarlet stockings and leather shoes, and the white kitten, and that I go to school and have coral beads, he will think I am the luckiest girl in the world."

"We will write him all that," said Captain Enos.

Just then the wooden latch of the kitchen door rattled and the door swung open.

"It's Amanda!" exclaimed Anne, and Amanda Cary stepped inside and carefully closed the door behind her.

"See, Amanda!" exclaimed Anne happily, "I have had a fine present. Mistress Starkweather gave me these," and she touched the pink beads, "and this!" and she pointed to the sweet-smelling box of sandalwood.

Amanda's thin face brightened. "I've got some coral beads just like yours," she said; "my father got them 'way off across the ocean. When I grow older and times are better, my mother says I shall have a white dress and can wear my coral beads then."

The two little girls played with the doll and kitten and Capain Enos kept on with his work.

"I wish I had a doll," he heard Amanda say. "I have asked Amos to make me one, but he is not clever at whittling out such things."

Captain Enos nodded to himself smilingly. Since Anne and Amos and Amanda had been carried down the harbor to House Point Island together, and he had heard how pleasant Amanda had been to Anne, he had liked the Cary children better, and had quite forgiven their old-time teasing ways. After Amanda had started for home he called Anne to him and said, "I have another secret!"

"Yes!" said Anne, with a gay little laugh.

"Would you like to make Amanda Cary a present?" he questioned.

"I could not give her my doll," answered Anne, her bright face growing sober, " 'Tis all I have that my father made."

"But if I make another doll, a fine wooden doll, as near like yours as I can, would you like to give that to Amanda?" asked Uncle Enos.

"Oh, yes! Yes, indeed," said Anne, the smiles all coming back again.

"Then 'tis a secret till I have the doll finished," said Captain Enos; "then maybe you can make a dress for it, and give it to Amanda, just as she gave you her white kitten."

Anne was very happy over this secret; it seemed even better than the new wooden chair for Martha Stoddard Nelson.

"I never gave anybody a present," she said, "but I know it must be the finest thing in the world to give somebody a gift," and she looked up into Uncle Enos's kindly face questioningly.

"You are a good child, Anne," he said, "and I will make the wooden doll as soon as time offers. Now take thy beads and box and Martha Stoddard Nelson to thy room, and I will bring in some wood for Aunt Martha. Then 'twill be time for a bite of supper."

Anne carried her treasures up-stairs to the little room. There was a stand in the room now, one that had belonged to her father. It had two drawers, and in one of them Anne carefully put the sandalwood box with the pink coral beads.

"I guess I have more lovely things then any little girl," she said to herself, as she slowly closed the drawer. "There's my doll, and my white kitten, and my scarlet stockings, which I shall have finished to-morrow, and my leather shoes, and these coral beads and the box!" But Anne gave a little sigh and then whispered, "And if my dear father could only know all about them, and that I am to give a doll to Amanda." She looked out of the small window toward the beautiful harbor, and wished that she might go sailing over it to Boston, to find her father and bring him safe to Provincetown. "I wish King George knew how much trouble he was making with his old war-ships," Anne whispered to the wooden doll.

CHAPTER XII

AN UNEXPECTED JOURNEY

"I HAVE a fine dish of ink all ready," said Captain Enos the next morning, "but 'tis too clear a morning to sit in the house and write letters. There are good cod coming into the harbor, and I must row out and catch what I can while the weather is good."

"Can we not write the letter to-night?" asked Anne. "Aunt Martha has some fine pitch knots to burn that will make the kitchen light as day."

"We'll see, come night," replied Captain Enos.

The two were walking down the sandy path together,—Captain Enos bound for the shore, and Anne started for Mistress Starkweather's to thank her for the coral beads.

"Be a good child," said Captain Enos, as he turned from the path and left Anne to go on alone.

As the little girl came near the spring, she saw a man rolling a water cask toward it, and toward the shore she could see several other men, whom she knew came from the British ship. She looked closely at the man at the spring, and as she passed near him, noticed that his hair was red. He smiled and nodded as Anne went by, and then she saw that he had pleasant blue eyes, and she stopped and said: "Have you forgotten the little girl you saved from the Indians?"

"No, indeed!" replied the big man heartily; "and so you are John Nelson's little girl. And you are not afraid of a Britisher?"

"Oh, no!" said Anne, in surprise; "you have two little maids in England."

"That I have, safe with their mother. But I should like well to see their bright faces, and your father would like to see you, child. You do not forget him?"

"No," said Anne soberly. "We plan to write him a letter for you to take."

"Speak not so loud," cautioned the man; "the other sailors may hear. And get your letter ready soon, for, come a fair wind, we'll be off up the coast again to Boston Harbor."

"Do your little girls write you letters?" asked Anne.

The big man shook his head. "No, they are not yet taught to write," he said. "It may be I'll be sailing back come spring, and then I'll tell them about the little maid I saw in Provincetown."

"Tell them my name is Anne," said she eagerly. "I wish I could go to Boston and find my father. I must hurry now, but I wish I knew the names of your little girls."

"They have good names," said the big man. "Each one is named for a grandmother. One is Betsey and the other Hannah."

"I'll remember," said Anne, and she said "Good-bye" and went quickly on toward Mrs. Stark-weather's.

"I do wish I could go and find my father," she thought as she walked along. "I know he'd like to see me better than a letter. I wish I had asked William Trull to take me in the big ship. But maybe Aunt Martha would not wish me to ask him."

All day Anne thought about the letter that Captain Enos had promised to write for her; and when supper was over and the kitchen began to grow dusky with the shadows of the October evening, she ran out to the little shed and came tugging in a big root of pine.

"May I put this on the fire, Aunt Martha?" she asked, "that Uncle Enos may see to write?"

" 'Tis a pine knot," said Mrs. Stoddard. "We shall need many such for light and heat before the long winter goes. But put it on, child. 'Tis a good plan to write thy father."

The pine knot blazed up brightly, and Captain Enos drew the table near the open fire, and, with Anne perched on a high stool beside him, and Mrs. Stoddard busy with her knitting, while the white kitten purred happily from its comfortable place under her chair, the letter was begun. Word for word, just as Anne told him, Captain Enos wrote down about the stockings and shoes, the school and the kitten, the pink beads and William Trull, and at last Anne said: "That is all, only that I want to see him and that I love him well," and Captain Enos finished the letter, and Anne went up-stairs to bed.

"I have a plan to take a cargo of fish to Boston, Martha," said Captain Enos, as soon as Anne had gone. "The 'Somerset' will sail on the first fair wind. I can fill the sloop with good cod by the time she is out of gunshot; and I'll venture to say they will bring a good price in Boston Town."

"But how can you make safe landing there, Enos?" asked his wife anxiously.

"I'll manage," replied the captain smilingly, "and it may be I can get some news of Anne's father."

" 'Twould be a brave cruise," said Mrs. Stoddard. "I should like well to go with thee, Enos."

Captain Enos laughed heartily. "And so would Anne, I dare say," he replied. "Maybe when spring comes and the British have been sent home I'll take you and Anne to Boston on a pleasure trip. If I get a good price for my fish, I'll bring you home a warm shawl, Martha."

"Mind not about me, Enos, but get some good wool cloth, if you see the chance, to make Anne a dress.

She likes bright colors, and the Freemans will tell you where to purchase, and you may see some plaid or figured stuff that has good wearing in it. Three yards of good width will be a plenty."

"There's but little trading in Boston these days," replied Captain Enos; "there's a blight on the land, until we can make England give us fairer treatment. I do believe 'twill come to open war in Boston."

As they talked, Captain Enos was busy shaping the wooden doll which Anne was to give Amanda.

"I must finish this before I begin to plan for Boston," he said. "What did we do for pleasure, Martha, before Anne came to live with us? Why, we had not even a white kitten. And 'twas little enough I thought of whittling out dolls."

"Or I of knitting scarlet stockings," answered his wife. "Anne knits her stint each day, and will soon have hers done, but her second pair I am knitting for the child. November is close at hand, and then she must be warmly clad."

"Her leather shoes are ready," said Captain Enos, with a satisfied nod.

The next morning Captain Enos gave the letter to William Trull, who promised to find a chance of forwarding it to John Nelson.

"What think you, Anne?" said Mrs. Stoddard when the little girl came home from school that day.

"The 'Somerset' is getting under way, and your Uncle Enos says 'tis like enough that your father will have the letter before the week ends."

"I wish I could see him read it," said Anne.

"And your Uncle Enos has a bold plan, child. He is filling up his sloop with fine cod to take to the Boston market, and if this wind holds, he will go sailing up the coast to-morrow morning. Mayhap he'll be in Boston before the 'Somerset.'"

"But they will fire their big guns at him and sink the sloop!" said Anne fearfully.

"Your uncle will not give them a chance," answered Mrs. Stoddard. "He will put in and out among the islands and keep out of their sight."

"May I not go with him, Aunt Martha? I could see my father then."

Mrs. Stoddard shook her head. "'Twould not be wise, child. Your uncle would not wish it. There would be but little chance of finding your father. Your uncle plans to make but a short stay and get home as soon as may be. It is no time to be coasting about, with British ships ready to sink any craft they see. Here, see!" and she held something up in her hand.

"Oh, Amanda's doll!" exclaimed Anne, "and you have made a fine dress for her. Can I take it down now?" and the little girl took the wooden doll which

Captain Enos had whittled out and looked at it admiringly.

"Yes, run along," replied Mrs. Stoddard; " 'twill be a great surprise for Amanda."

Anne hurried down the hill and along the shore toward the Cary house, holding the doll carefully under the little shawl of gay plaid which Mrs. Stoddard had pinned about her shoulders. The sand no longer felt warm about her bare feet.

"I shall be wearing my new stockings and shoes soon," she thought, as her feet felt the cold dampness.

Amanda saw her coming and ran out to meet her, a white kitten close at her heels.

"See, the British ship is going!" exclaimed Amanda, and the two little girls turned and watched the big ship under full sail moving off across the harbor.

"Amanda," said Anne, "you know you gave me the nice white kitten?"

"Yes," replied Amanda; "has it run away?"

"Oh, no; it is just as contented as can be," said Anne; "only ever since you gave it to me I have wished I could give you something."

Amanda's face flushed and she dug her bare toes into the sand. She was remembering how unkind she and Amos had been to Anne, and was wishing that Anne would not thank her for the kitten.

"And now I have a present for you," went on Anne, taking the wooden doll from beneath the little plaid shawl.

"Your doll!" exclaimed Amanda in surprise.

Anne shook her head smilingly.

"No," she said, "your doll. See, it is new. And it is larger than mine. Take it," for Amanda's hands were behind her, as if she did not mean to take the gift.

"It's yours. Uncle Enos made it, and Aunt Martha made the dress," and Anne held the doll toward her friend.

Then Amanda's hands unclasped and reached forward eagerly.

"It's a fine doll," she said. "I do think, Anne, it is full handsomer than yours. Come, that I may show it to my mother. I shall name it for you, Anne. I have already named it. I shall call it Lovely Anne Nelson. Indeed I shall. I never had a gift before." And Amanda held the doll tight and smiled happily at Anne, as she reached out to draw her into the house that Mrs. Cary might see the doll.

When Anne started for home, Amanda walked along beside her for a little way. When they neared the spring she put her arm about Anne's neck and kissed her on the cheek.

"There!" she exclaimed; "now you know how dear you are. I was bad to you, Anne Nelson, right here at this very spring; and I set Amos on to tease you. And now you have given me a gift."

"But you gave me the kitten," answered Anne, "and I chased you away from the spring with sand and water."

"But now we like each other well," said Amanda. "You like me now, Anne?"

"Yes," replied the little girl; "I would not give you a gift if I did not like you well," and the two little girls smiled at each other happily and parted, Amanda to run home to her doll, while Anne went more slowly up the hill, thinking of the trip Uncle Enos was about to make and wishing that she could go with him.

"I could wear my scarlet stockings and new shoes for my father to see," she thought, "and I would be no trouble to Uncle Enos. There are two bunks in the sloop's cabin, and I would be company for him."

The more Anne thought about this cruise to Boston the more she longed to go. Captain Enos was late to his supper that night.

"I have a fine cargo of fish," he said, "and I shall go out on the morning tide, before you are awake, little maid," with a nod to Anne. "Next spring you and Aunt Martha shall go with me and see the fine town of Boston, with its shops and great houses. The British soldiers will be gone by that time, and it may be we will have our own government. There will be good days for us all then."

"I want to go now," said Anne, and Captain Enos laughed and shook his head.

"Run away to bed now, child," said Aunt Martha, as soon as the supper dishes were washed, "and take these stockings up-stairs with you. I toed off the last one while you were at Amanda Cary's."

So Anne said good-night, and Captain Enos gave her a good-bye kiss, telling her to take good care of her Aunt Martha while he was away, and went slowly up-stairs. But she did not undress and go to bed. She sat down on the little wooden stool, her mind full of a great resolve. She sat there quietly until she heard Captain Enos and Mrs. Stoddard go to bed. Then she moved softly to the little table under which stood her new shoes. Taking these and her scarlet stocking, she crept softly down the stairs. Crossing the kitchen gently, she slid back the bolt, and let herself out into the night.

There was a fresh wind from the southwest, and the little girl shivered a little as she ran toward the shore. The sloop was anchored some little distance from shore; Captain Enos would row out in his dory to her. As Anne reached the shore and looked out at the sloop she almost lost courage.

"I don't see how I can ever get out there without a boat," she exclaimed aloud.

"Out there?" the voice sounded close at her elbow, and Anne gave a jump and looked around.

"What do you want to get out to Captain Enos's boat for?" asked Jimmie Starkweather.

"Oh, Jimmie!" exclaimed the little girl, "what are you doing down on the shore in the night?"

"Night! Why, it's not much after dark" answered the boy. "Father has been out fishing all day, and I have just pulled the dory up, and was going home when I heard you. What do you want to go out to the sloop for?"

"Jimmie, my father is in Boston and I do want to see him," said Anne. "Captain Enos is going to sail early to-morrow morning for Boston, and I want to go out and sleep in the cabin to-night. Then I will keep as quiet as I can till he is nearly in Boston, and then I will tell him all about it, and he will take me to see my father."

Jimmie shook his head.

"Doesn't Captain Enos want you to go?" he asked.

"He says I may go next spring," answered Anne, "but if you row me out to the sloop, Jimmie, 'twould be no harm. You could tell Aunt Martha to-morrow, and I would soon be home. But 'tis a long time since I saw my father. You see yours every day."

There was a little sob in Anne's throat and Jimmie wondered if she was going to cry. He hoped she wouldn't.

"Jump into the dory," he said. "I'll get a good lesson from my father, I'll warrant, for this; but jump in. And mind you tell Captain Enos that I told you to go home, but that you would not."

"Yes, Jimmie," said Anne, putting her shoes and stockings into the boat, and then climbing in herself. The boy sprang in after her, pushed off the dory, and in a short time had reached the sloop.

"Now go straight to the cabin and shut the door," cautioned Jimmie, and Anne obeyed, creeping into the top bunk and pulling a rough blanket over her.

She heard the sound of Jimmie's oars, as he pulled toward shore, felt the motion of the tide, as the big sloop rose and fell, and soon was asleep and dreaming that her father and William Trull were calling her a brave little maid.

Jimmie had many misgivings after he reached shore, and made up his mind to go straight to Captain Stoddard and tell him of Anne's plan. Then he remembered that Anne had trusted him with her secret. "I guess I'll have to let her go," he decided.

CHAPTER XIII

ANNE FINDS HER FATHER

It was just daybreak when Captain Enos, carrying a basket of provisions for his cruise, made his way to the shore and pushed off his dory.

"Not a soul stirring," he said, as he stepped aboard the sloop, fastened the dory, which he intended to tow, and then carried the basket of food to the little cabin.

As he pushed open the door Anne awoke, but she did not stir, and Captain Enos did not look in the direction of the upper bunk. She heard him hoisting the big mainsail, then came the rattle of the anchor chain, the sloop swung round, and Anne knew that at last she was really on her way to find her father.

"I must keep very still," she whispered to herself, "or Uncle Enos might 'bout ship and sail straight back to Provincetown," so she did not move, though she wished very much that she might be out on deck with Captain Enos, feeling the salt breeze on her cheeks and enjoying the sail. She knew by the way the sloop tipped that they were going very fast.

"Seems as if it was sailing right on its side," thought Anne; "if it tips much more I do believe I'll slide out of this berth."

"A fine wind, a fine wind!" Captain Enos said with a satisfied nod, as his boat went flying along; "I'll make Boston Harbor before nightfall at this rate, in time to get my fish ashore by dusk, if I can slide into a landing without the British stopping me. My cargo will be welcome," and Captain Enos smiled to himself as he thought of the praise he would get from his friends and acquaintances for his brave venture in such troublous times.

Toward noon Anne carefully let herself down from the bunk, and peered out through the door, which Captain Enos had left open. She could see the low sandy shores of Cape Cod, and here and there a white-sailed boat. "I guess we must be 'most to Boston," she thought; "the sun is way up in the middle of the sky, and I am so hungry." She came a little nearer to the cabin door and put her head out. "Uncle Enos!" she said softly.

But the captain was singing to keep himself company, and did not hear the faint voice. His head was turned a little away from Anne, but just as she was about to call him again his song came to an end and he turned his glance ahead.

"Bless my soul!" he exclaimed.

"It is I, Uncle Enos!" said Anne, stepping out of the cabin.

The captain was almost too surprised to speak. Anne clambered along the side of the sloop until she was close beside him, and reaching out took fast hold of his rough coat sleeve, and repeated:

"It is I, Uncle Enos."

"Where on earth did you come from?" he exclaimed.

Anne pointed toward the cabin.

"How did you get there?" questioned Captain Enos. "Weren't you abed and asleep when I left the house this morning?"

"No, Uncle Enos," said Anne, creeping a little closer; "I slept in the top bunk in the sloop."

"Well, this is a nice affair. I can't take you back now. I'll make Boston Harbor before dusk with this wind. But how came you in the sloop?"

"Jimmie Starkweather rowed me out last night after you were sound asleep. And he is going to tell Aunt Martha all about it this morning. He told me to tell you that he didn't want me to go aboard, but that I would," said Anne.

Captain Enos's face was very sober, but he did not say any harsh word.

"What did you hide in the sloop for, child?" he asked.

"To go to Boston with you, Uncle Enos, and find my father," said Anne.

Then the captain's face grew even more sober.

"Then you do not like living with us?" he said; but I thought you seemed happy, Anne. Your Aunt Martha will miss you, child. But if your heart is so set on being with your father I must do my best to find him for you. How a soldier can manage to care for a small girl like you is more than I can tell," and the captain sighed.

"I brought my scarlet stockings and new shoes to show him," said Anne.

Captain Enos nodded.

"And I can tell him about my kitten and the coral beads, and about going to school."

"Did you not bring the coral beads?" asked the captain.

Anne shook her head.

"Oh, no," she answered "I heard you tell Aunt Martha that you would be away but a day or two, and I thought I could tell my father about the beads."

"Then you mean to go home with me?" asked the captain, a little smile creeping about his mouth.

"Why, yes," said Anne. "I do but want to see my father and tell him all the pleasant things that have befallen me."

"Well, well," said Captain Enos, "now I must scold you, Anne. Your Aunt Martha will not be pleased at this."

"But you are not angry?" asked Anne. "I do see little wrinkles about your eyes that mean you will soon smile. And it is long since I have seen my father."

"We must make the best of it now," said the captain, "but I do blame the Starkweather boy for setting you out to the sloop. He should have sent you straight home, and let me know of your plan."

Anne looked at Captain Enos in surprise.

"Jimmie could not help my coming," she said. "I should have found some way to get to the sloop. And he would not tell a secret."

"So you did not mean to run away from us?" said Captain Enos. "I am glad of that, but how I will manage with you in Boston I know not, nor if I can find your father."

Captain Enos's sloop ran safely in among the islands, sailed across Boston Harbor without being noticed, and made fast at a wharf well known to Captain Enos, and where he was welcomed by an old acquaintance. Before dusk he had sold his cargo of fish at a good price, and Anne, wearing her scarlet stockings and new shoes, and holding fast to the captain's hand, walked with him up the street to the house of the man who had been at the wharf when the sloop came in.

"They are good people, born in Wellfleet," said the captain to Anne, as they walked along, "and I shall ask them to keep you over night. I shall sleep in the sloop, and tomorrow we will find out all we can about your father."

The Freemans, for that was the name of Captain Enos's friends, gave Anne a warm welcome. Their house seemed very large and grand to the little girl. There was a carpet on the sitting-room floor, the first Anne had ever seen, and pictures on the walls, and a high mantel with tall brass candlesticks.

The room in which she slept seemed very wonderful to Anne. The bed was so high that she had to step up from a footstool to get in it, and then down, down she went in billows of feathers. In the morning one of the Freeman girls came in to waken her. She was a girl of about fifteen, with pretty, light, curling hair and blue eyes. She smiled pleasantly at Anne, and told her that there was a basin of warm water for her to bathe her face and hands in.

"I will brush out your hair for you, if you wish," she said kindly.

But Anne said she could brush her own hair. Rose Freeman waited till Anne was quite ready for breakfast and went down the broad flight of stairs with her. Anne watched her new friend admiringly.

"She looks just like her name, just like a rose," she said to herself, and resolved that she would remember and walk just as Rose did, and try and speak in the same pleasant way.

Before breakfast was finished Captain Enos came up from the wharves. He smiled as he looked at Anne's bright face and smooth hair, and nodded approvingly. Then he and Mr. Freeman began to talk about the soldiers, and the best way to find John Nelson.

"Come, Rose," said Mr. Freeman; "the captain and I will walk up near King's Chapel and see what we can find out, and you and the little maid can come with us."

Rose went up-stairs and came down wearing a little brown jacket and a hat of brown silk with a green feather on it. In her hands she brought a blue cape and a blue hat with a broad ribbon bow.

"Mother says you are to wear these," she said to Anne, with a little smile; " 'tis a cape and hat that I wore when I was a little girl, and I would like to have you wear them."

"I never wore a hat before," said Anne.

"It is very becoming," said Rose, and the little party started out.

Mr. Freeman stopped here and there to ask questions, and Anne, holding fast to Rose Freeman's hand, looked wonderingly at the houses and the people. They went into a shop, and Captain Enos bought a fine warm brown shawl to take home to Mrs. Stoddard, and asked Rose Freeman to help Anne select a pretty stuff for a dress. The girls decided upon a small plaid of dark blue and brown, and the stuff was carefully wrapped up and Captain Enos took the package.

"I have news at last," said Mr. Freeman, who had been talking with a man at the door of the shop. "We will walk up to the Common and see if we cannot get sight of your father. He was here yesterday."

Anne listened eagerly, almost forgetting Rose Freeman, whose hand she still held tightly, in the thought that her dear father might be very near and that she would soon see him.

They walked toward the Common, and Mr. Freeman told the others to stand near the big elm while he went to make inquiries. He was gone but a few moments, when Rose Freeman felt Anne's hand slip from her own, and saw the little girl running swiftly across the grass calling out, "Father! Father!"

John Nelson heard the voice and stopped.

"Anne, Anne!" he answered, and in a moment the little girl in scarlet stockings and blue cape and hat was gathered into the close clasp of the dark, slender man.

Then how much there was to say! How eagerly Anne told him all the pleasant news! How warmly Captain Enos shook his hand, and called him a brave fellow; and John Nelson tried to thank the captain for all his kindness to Anne.

Anne held fast to his hand as they walked together to the wharf where the sloop lay. Captain Enos said that he must start for home the next morning, and there was a great deal for them all to talk about. Rose Freeman and her father left them at the wharf, after Captain Enos had promised that he would bring Anne to their house in time for supper.

"I have a plan, John," said Captain Enos; "when we have settled with the British, and that must be soon now, you must come to Provincetown and live with us. How would you like that, Anne?"

Anne smiled happily.

"Best of anything!" she declared.

"I need help with my fishing," went on Captain Enos, "and there's an empty loft next to Anne's room, where you can sleep. So think of Anne's home as yours, John. You'd not break Mistress Stoddard's heart by taking away the child?"

"It was good fortune led her to your door," said John Nelson gratefully. "I can see for myself that she is content and happy. And I'll be a fortunate man to come into your house, Enos Stoddard."

"How soon will you come, father?" asked Anne, hopefully.

"I think 'twill not be longer than another spring before the British leave us in peace," replied her father. "But we need more soldiers to let them know we are ready for war."

Captain Enos nodded. "There's a half dozen good Provincetown men ready to come, and as many more from Truro, if a dozen would help," he found a chance to whisper.

"We'll talk of this later," said Anne's father. "I only hope you'll get safe back to Provincetown harbor from this trip."

"No fear," laughed Captain Enos. "General Gage is doing his best to starve Boston out. Maybe we Provincetown men can do the cause of Liberty good service if we can bring in loads of fish for the people."

"It's hard to have British troops quartered on us," replied Nelson. "General Gage is taking rough measures with everybody who opposes him. Dr. Joseph Warren tried to stop the fortifications on Boston Neck, but 'twas no use. And word is being sent to settlements to be ready to furnish men. We've got supplies in Concord, and Americans have been drilling for some time. We'll be ready for war if war comes. I've a message for the Newburyport men to be ready to join us, but I see no way of getting out of Boston. You're a brave man, Captain Stoddard, to come into harbor."

Captain Enos's face brightened as he listened to John Nelson.

"I'd find no trouble in slipping down the coast to Newburyport," he said eagerly.

"Maybe," responded Nelson, "tho' there's no need for my telling you that there's British craft cruising all about, and a man caught with a message to 'rebels,' as they call us, stands no chance."

"I'd keep my message to myself," answered Captain Enos.

"So you could, a message by word of mouth; but this is written, and has a drawing as well. I have it under the lining of my coat. But there's no way for me to get out of the town. I'm well known by many of the English."

"Let me take it." Captain Stoddard's voice was eager. " 'Tis ill-luck that we Provincetown men are to have no part in this affair. I'll get the paper safe to Newburyport. Tell me to whom I am to give it."

But John Nelson shook his head. "You'd be caught, and maybe sent to England," he answered.

"I'll not be caught. And if they catch me they'd not find the papers," he promised, and before they parted

Nelson had agreed to deliver the package that day. "I'll give it to Anne," he promised. "It will not do for me to meet you again. There are too many eyes about. Let Anne walk along,with that tall girl yonder, about sunset toward the South Meeting House, and I'll give it to her."

Captain Stoddard nodded, and walked away.

"Anne," he said when they met in the Freemans' sitting-room just before dinner, "you can be of great help to your father and to me. But you must be wise and silent. When you walk with Rose this afternoon your father will meet you and hand you a flat package. Thrust it inside your frock, and say nothing of it to Rose, or to any one, and bring it safe to me."

"Yes, indeed, Uncle Enos," the little girl answered. "Am I to ask Rose to walk with me?"

"Yes, toward the South Meeting House," answered Captain Enos, "about an hour before sunset."

"If I keep silent and bring the package safely, will you forgive me for hiding in the boat?" pleaded Anne.

"Indeed I will, child, and take you for a brave girl as well," he replied.

Anne was joyful at the thought of another word from her father, and Rose was quite ready to go for another walk.

They had just turned into King Street when John Nelson met them. Anne wore the pretty cape Rose had given her and her father slipped the packet into her hand without Rose seeing it. She grasped it tightly, and held it under the cape. "Be a good child, Anne, and do whatever Captain Stoddard may bid thee," her father said as he bade her good-bye.

CHAPTER XIV

A CANDY PARTY

THE next morning proved warm and pleasant with only a light breeze, but Captain Enos had his sloop ready at an early hour, and when Anne, with Mr. Freeman and Rose, came down to the wharf he was anxious to start at once.

Anne still wore the blue cape, which Mrs. Freeman had insisted on giving her, and the hat was in a round pasteboard box, which Anne carried carefully, and which was put away in the cabin with Aunt Martha's new shawl and the cloth for Anne's new dress.

As the sloop sailed away from the wharf Anne waved her hand to Rose Freeman until she could no longer see her. Captain Enos watched the little girl anxiously; he was half afraid that Anne might be disappointed because she could not stay with her father, but her face was bright and smiling.

"Where is the packet your father handed you?" Captain Enos questioned eagerly, as soon as his sloop was clear of the wharf.

"I have it pinned safe inside my frock," she answered. "Shall I give it to you now, Uncle Enos?"

"Maybe 'tis safer with you, Anne," replied the captain. "It may be that some British boat will overhaul us, and question us. I'm doing an errand, Anne, for your father. If this boat is taken and I am made a prisoner, you are to say that you want to go to Newburyport. That and no more. Mayhap they'll set you ashore there. Then make your way to Squire Coffin's house as best you may. Give him the packet. Tell him the story, and he'll find a way to reach your father. Do you understand?"

"Yes, Uncle Enos," said Anne very soberly.

"Repeat what I have told you, that I may be sure," said Captain Enos, and Anne obeyed.

"But I do not want to be set ashore in a strange place," she said soberly. "How should I get back to Provincetown?"

"You will be taken care of, never fear," responded Captain Enos, "and you'll be doing a good service to the cause of liberty, Anne, if you carry the papers safely. Your Aunt Martha will indeed be proud of you. Remember what I have told you. But I hope to slip in behind Plum Island and make a landing without being seen. The wind is favoring us. You have had a fine visit, Anne?"

"Yes, indeed!" agreed the little girl, "and I have a present for Aunt Martha," she said, as the sloop ran out among the islands. "See, my father gave me this for her," and she held up a gold coin. "Will she not be pleased?"

"But she will be better pleased to have you safe home again," said Captain Enos. "What do you think Amanda Cary will say when she hears of your voyage to Boston and of all the fine things you have seen there? 'Tis not many of the children in Provincetown have ever taken such a journey."

"She will think it a better voyage than the one we took to House Point Island," answered Anne. "I have something for Amanda, too. Rose Freeman gave me a package of barley sugar, and I said to myself I would take it home to Amanda."

Captain Enos kept a watchful eye for suspicious looking craft. But his course lay well in-shore, and he was apparently not noticed by any of the vessels. Before noon he was cruising along the Ipswich shore, and made his landing at Newburyport without having been spoken.

"The worst part of the business is before us," he said to Anne, as he made the boat fast. "If I leave the boat here, I may come back and find no trace of her, but leave her I must, or Squire Coffin will wait in vain for the papers."

"But I can carry them," said Anne. "Tell me where to go, and I'll come straight back and say no word of my errand."

" 'Tis the best possible way. Did I not say that you were a wise child!" declared Captain Enos, his face beaming with delight. "Put on your pretty hat and cape, and follow that lane up to the main road. Then ask for Squire Coffin's house of the first person you meet."

In a few moments Anne was ready to start. As she walked up the lane Captain Enos's eyes followed her anxiously. "I can see no danger in it for the child," he said aloud, and then, sailor fashion, set about putting his boat in order.

"'Twill be a cold night, but the cabin will be snug and warm," he thought. "I'll get out of here before sunset and maybe make Provincetown by daybreak."

Anne walked up the pleasant lane. Her feet sank deep in the leaves from the overarching trees, and made a cheerful, crackling sound. She could see the roofs of houses not far away, and as she turned from the lane into a road she met two girls not much larger than herself. They looked at her curiously, and when Anne stopped they smiled in a friendly way.

"Would you please to tell me where I can find Squire Coffin?" Anne asked, feeling very brave and a little important.

"Squire Coffin is my uncle," the larger of the two girls replied. "I'm going there now."

"I have an errand," Anne explained.

"Oh!" responded both the little girls, but Anne could see that they wondered who this strange little girl could be, and what her errand was.

"You may come with us if you want to," Squire Coffin's niece said, and Anne was very glad to walk with these silent little girls, for neither of them spoke again until they stopped in front of a tall, square white house very near the street. As Anne looked up at it she thought that she had never seen so many windows before in one house. "That's Uncle Coffin on the porch," explained his niece.

"Thank you," said Anne, and as the two little girls politely curtseyed she endeavored to imitate them, and with apparent success. Then she went up the stone steps toward the dignified looking gentleman who stood in the doorway.

She held the packet under her cape, and as she came near him she whispered, as Captain Enos had told her to do, "This is from Boston."

"Great George!" he exclaimed grabbing the package, in what seemed a very rude manner to Anne, and putting it quickly in his pocket, "and how came you by it?"

But Anne remembered her promise to keep quiet, and she also remembered that the squire's niece had made the queer little curtsey on saying good-bye. So

"THIS IS FROM BOSTON"

Anne bobbed very prettily to the squire, and said "good-bye," and ran down the steps, leaving the squire standing amazed. It was many weeks before he learned the name of the little maid, and that her home was in Provincetown.

It was an easy matter to find her way back to the lane. There was an orchard just at the corner of the road, and a man was gathering apples. "Want an apple?" he called.

"Yes, sir," answered Anne, and now, being rather proud of her new accomplishment, she curtseyed very politely.

"Well, well, you are a young lady, miss. Come up to the fence and I'll hand you the apples." Anne obeyed, and the good-natured man gave her two big red-cheeked apples. They seemed very wonderful to the little girl from the sandy shore village, where apples were not often to be seen, and she thanked him delightedly.

Captain Enos was watching for her, and as soon as she was on board he swung the sloop clear of the wharf, ran up his mainsail and headed toward the outer channel. As they looked back at the little wharf they saw a tall man come running down the lane.

"I reckon that's the squire," chuckled Captain Enos.

"Yes, it is," said Anne.

"Well, now for Provincetown. I guess we've helped a little bit, Anne. At least you have. "

Anne was eating one of the big red apples, and thinking about Squire Coffin's big house and small niece.

"We'll tell Aunt Martha all that's happened," went on Captain Enos, "but do not speak to any one else of it, Anne. 'Twould make trouble for your father and for me if our trip to Newburyport was known."

"I'll not speak of it," Anne promised.

"It has been a good trip," said Captain Enos. "Mr. Freeman paid we well for the fish. I have a keg of molasses in the cabin, which will be welcome news for Martha."

As they came into harbor at sunrise next morning and Captain Enos dropped anchor and lowered the big mainsail, Anne looked eagerly toward the shore. She could see Jimmie Starkweather and his father watching them. After Captain Enos had lowered the keg of molasses into the dory, and put in the box that held Anne's hat, and the other packages, he helped Anne over the side of the sloop to a seat in the bow of the dory.

As soon as the boat touched the shore Jimmie and his father ran down to help draw it up on the beach. Jimmie looked at Captain Enos as if he half expected a scolding, but as soon as Captain Enos landed he patted the boy's shoulder kindly, and said:

"The little maid has told me all about it. You were not greatly to blame, Jimmie. And the trip turned out all right."

"I saw my father," said Anne, and then ran away toward home, leaving Captain Enos to tell of the visit to Boston.

Aunt Martha had seen the sloop come to anchor, and was waiting at the door to welcome Anne.

"Uncle Enos and I have a secret with my father," Anne whispered to Mrs. Stoddard, "and we have been to Newburyport." And then the story of the wonderful trip was told, and Anne showed Mrs. Stoddard how she had cursteyed to the squire.

"Well! Well!" exclaimed the good woman in amazement. "It does seem as if you had all sorts of adventures, Anne. To think of Enos undertaking such a thing. I'm proud of you both. 'Twill be a fine story to tell your grandchildren, Anne. How you carried news from Boston patriots to Newburyport. But do not speak of it till we are through with all these troublous days." And again Anne promised to keep silent.

"To think you should run off like that, child," continued Aunt Martha. "When Jimmie Starkweather came up and told me you were gone I could scarce believe him till I had climbed the stairs to the loft and found no trace of you. But I am right glad you wore your shoes and stockings. Where did the blue cape come from?

By this time they were in the kitchen, and Anne had put down the box that held her hat.

"Mrs. Freeman gave it to me," she replied, "and see! I have a new hat!" and she opened the box and took out the pretty hat.

"I thought thy uncle would take thee straight to Mistress Freeman," said Mrs. Stoddard.

"And we found my father," went on Anne happily, "and he sent thee this," and she drew the gold piece from her pocket and gave it to Mrs. Stoddard.

"Well, well," said Aunt Martha, " 'tis a fine piece of money, and your father is kind to send it. I will use it well."

"And Uncle Enos has fetched you a fine shawl and a keg of molasses," said Anne. "You do not think there was great harm in my hiding in the sloop, Aunt Martha?" The little girl's face was so troubled that Aunt Martha her her another kiss, and said:

"It has turned out well, but thee must never do so again. Suppose a great storm had come up and swept the sloop from her moorings that night?"

"Rose Freeman looks just like a rose," said Anne, feeling quite sure that Aunt Martha was not displeased; "and she walks so softly that you can hardly hear her, and she speaks softly, too. I am going to walk and speak just as she does."

"That is right," agreed Mrs. Stoddard. "I am sure that she is a well-spoken girl."

When Captain Enos came up the hill toward home Anne had already put her blue cape and hat carefully away, and was sitting near the fire with the white kitten curled up in her lap.

"The Freemans do not eat in their kitchen," said Anne, as they sat down to supper; "they eat in a square room with a shining floor, and where there is a high mantel-shelf with china images."

" 'Tis a fine house," agreed Captain Enos, "well built of brick. 'Twas a great thing for Anne to see it."

" 'Tis not so pleasant a house as this," said Anne. "I could not see the harbor from any window, and the shore is not smooth and sandy like the shores of our harbor."

Captain Enos smiled and nodded.

"That's right, Anne," he said; "Boston houses may do for town people, but we sailor-folk like our own best."

"Yes, indeed!" replied Anne, "and I do not believe a beach-plum grows on their shore. And nothing

I tasted there was so good as Aunt Martha's meal bread."

The next morning Anne started for school, wearing the new shoes and scarlet stockings and the little plaid shawl. The childen were all anxious to hear about what she saw in Boston, and she told them of the soldiers on the Common, and of the shops, and of the houses made of brick and stone, and she showed Amanda how to make the wonderful curtsey. But Elder Haven soon called them to take their seats, and it was not until the noon recess that she found a chance to speak alone with Amanda.

The two little girls sat down on the front door-step of Elder Haven's house, and Anne told of the wonderful sail to Boston, and had just begun to describe Rose Freeman when the teacher's voice was heard calling them in.

As soon as school closed for the day, Amanda said that she could walk home with Anne and see the new cape and hat, and hear more about Rose Freeman.

"Would you like better to live in Boston than here?" asked Amanda, as they walked along.

Anne looked at her in surprise.

"Why, Amanda!" she said; "of course I wouldn't. It is not seemly there to go out-of-dooors without a hat; and Rose Freeman said that she had never been barefooted in her life. She has fine white stockings knit of cotton yarn for summer, and low shiny shoes that she called 'slippers.'"

"'Twould be hard to wear shoes all the year," agreed Amanda, looking down at her own stout leather shoes, "but I like them well now."

"I brought you a present from Boston," said Anne just as they reached the Stoddards' door. "Rose Freeman gave it to me, and I saved it for you."

"Well, Amanda," said Mrs. Stoddard, as the two girls came into the kitchen, "are you not glad to have Anne safe home again? 'Twas quite a journey to take."

"She likes Provincetown better than Boston," answered Amanda smilingly.

"To be sure she does, and why not?" replied Mrs. Stoddard. "There are few places where there is so much salt water to be seen as here, and no better place for fishing. Now, Anne, I have a little surprise for you. I have asked Mr. and Mrs. Starkweather and their six boys to come up this evening, and your father and mother, Amanda, and you and Amos. The evenings are getting fine and long now and we must begin to be neighborly."

"Then I mustn't stay long now," said Amanda; "it will be pleasant to come up here again in the evening."

Amanda tried on Anne's blue cape and hat, looked admiringly at Mrs. Stoddard's shining gold piece and brown shawl, and then Anne handed her the package of barley sugar.

"I will keep it," said Amanda, gratefully; "'twould seem ungrateful to eat a present."

Mrs. Stoddard nodded. "Keep it until Sunday, Amanda," she said, "but then it will be well to eat a part of it."

"But can she not taste it now?" asked Anne. "I am sure it is good. It came out of a big glass jar in a shop."

"I see I must tell you two little girls a secret," said Mrs. Stoddard, "but Amanda must not tell Amos."

"No, indeed," said Amanda quickly.

"It is about this evening," said Mrs. Stoddard; "I am going to make a fine dish of molasses candy!"

"Oh, Aunt Martha!" "Oh, Mistress Stoddard!" exclaimed the little girls together.

"It has been years since I tasted any myself," went on Mrs. Stoddard, "but I remember well how it is made; and I do not believe one of you children has ever tasted it."

"My mother has told us about it," said Amanda, "and said that when times were better she would make us some."

"We all need cheering up," said Mrs. Stoddard, "and I am glad I can give you children a treat to remember. Now, Amanda, you see why it will be best not to eat your barley sugar until Sunday."

"I have good times every day since I gave you the white kitten," said Amanda, as she bade Anne good-bye, and started for home

"We must bring all our chairs into the kitchen to-night, Anne," said Aunt Martha, as soon as supper was finished, "for even then I doubt if there be seats enough for your company."

"I had best bring in my long bench from the shed," said Captain Enos; " 'twill be just the thing to put a row of Starkweather boys on."

"The youngest is but two years old," said Mrs. Stoddard; " 'tis like he will find our bed a good resting place."

Mr. and Mrs. Cary with Amos and Amanda were the first to arrive, and as they came in Captain Enos put two big pieces of pitch pine on the fire. In a moment it blazed up making the kitchen as light as day.

The Starkweathers, climbing up the sandy hill, saw the bright light shining through the windows of the little house, and Mrs. Strarkweather exclaimed:

"Does it not look cheerful? To think of us all coming to a merrymaking! It was surely a kind thought of Mistress Stoddard's."

"Shall we play games?" asked Daniel, the boy next younger than Jimmie.

"It may be," answered his mother, and you boys must be quiet and not rough in your play. Remember there is a little girl in the house."

The youngest Starkweather boy, carried carefully by his father, was sound asleep when they reached the Stoddards', and was put comfortably down on Mrs. Stoddard's big bed, while the others gathered around the fire.

"Sit you here, boys," directed Captain Enos, pointing to the long bench. "and you girls can bring your stools beside me. I have a fine game for you to play. Do you see this shining brass button? 'Twas given me in Boston, and came from the coat of a British soldier. Now we will play 'Button' with it," and the captain, with a few whispered words to Jimmie Starkweather, slid the shining button into his hand, and "Button, button! who's got the button?" was soon being laughingly asked from one to another as the brass button went from Jimmie to Amos, passed into Anne's hand and swiftly on to Amanda, and back to Jimmie before Captain Enos could locate it.

"Look!" exclaimed one of the younger Starkweather boys. "Mistress Stoddard is pouring syrup into a kettle!"

"Yes, my boy," said Captain Enos laughingly, "and now you will all be glad that I had a good trip to Boston, for I brought home a keg of fine molasses, and now you will have some first-class candy!"

There were many exclamations of surprise and pleasure, even the older members of the party declaring that it would indeed be a fine treat; and

Mrs. Starkweather said that it reminded her of the times when she was a little girl like Anne, and her mother made candy for her.

The molasses boiled and bubbled in the big kettle hung over the fire, and Mrs. Stoddard and Mrs. Cary took turns in stirring it. The children brought dippers of cold water for spoonfuls of the hot molasses to be dropped in to see if it had begun to candy; and when Amanda lifted a stringy bit from her tin cup and held it up for Mrs. Stoddard to see, it was decided that it was cooked enough, and the kettle was lifted from the fire and the steaming, fragrant mass turned into carefully buttered pans.

"We must set these out-of-doors to cool," said Mrs. Stoddard; so Jimmie, Amos and Daniel were each entrusted with a pan to carry out on the broad step.

"When it is cool we will all work it," said Mrs. Stoddard; "that means pull and twist it into sticks."

It did not take long for the candy to cool, and then under Mrs. Stoddard's directions each child was given a piece to work into shape. But the candy proved too tempting to work over, and in a few minutes the long bench was filled with a row of boys, each one happily chewing away upon a clumsy piece of molasses candy.

CHAPTER XV

A SPRING PICNIC

BEFORE the six weeks of school came to an end Anne could read, and could write well enough to begin a letter to her father, although there seemed no chance of sending it. She thought often of her visit to Newburyport, and wondered if she would ever see Squire Coffin's little niece again. And she remembered William Trull, and his little daughters of whom he had told her. But no news had come to Provincetown of how Boston was faring.

A few weeks after Captain Enos's trip to Boston another Provincetown fisherman had started out with a cargo of fish, hoping for equal good fortune. But weeks passed and he did not return, and no tidings were heard of him, and his family and neighbors now feared that the British had captured his boat and taken him prisoner.

No word came to Anne from her father, and as the ice formed along the shore and over the brooks, the cold winds came sweeping in from sea with now and then a fall of snow that whitened the marshes and the woods, the little settlement on the end of Cape Cod was entirely shut off from news from Boston, and they knew not what the British were doing.

Captain Enos and the men of the port went fishing in the harbor, and the women and children kept snug at home in the little houses.

Captain Enos had finished the cedar chair for Anne's doll, and Amos had made one as near like it as possible for Amanda's "Lovely Anne." Both the little girls could now knit nearly as smoothly as Mrs. Stoddard herself, and almost every day Amanda came up to Mrs. Stoddard's, for she and Anne were reading "Pilgrim's Progress" together. Now and then Mrs. Stoddard would read several pages aloud of the adventures of Christian, while the two little girls knit. Anne had a warm hood of gray and scarlet yarn which she had knit herself, and mittens to match, so that she could go to church on Sundays, and run down to Mrs. Starkweather's or to see Amanda without being chilled by the cold.

It was a mild day late in February when Jimmie Starkweather brought home a pink blossom from the woods.

"See, mother! The first Mayflower," he exclaimed. "I found it half under the snow. Does it not smell sweet?"

"It does indeed, son," replied Mrs. Starkweather; "bring me your grandmother's pink china cup from the cupboard, fill it with cool water, and we will put the blossom on the table for thy father to see. Spring is indeed close at hand."

On the same day that Jimmie found the arbutus bloom, Captain Enos came in from fishing with news to tell. A Boston schooner outward bound had come near to where he was fishing, and in response to his hail and call of "What news?" had answered that a battle was now expected at any day between the British and Americans.

"If it be so," said Captain Enos, "'twill not be long before the British ships will be homeward bound, and they'll not stop to trouble us much on their way."

"We must keep a lookout for them," said Captain Starkweather. "I wish we could get more news. 'Tis like enough all will be settled before we know aught of it."

All through March, with its high winds and heavy rains the people watched the harbor for a sight of the big white-winged ships, knowing that if the English ships were homeward bound it would mean that the Americans had won, and that the colonies would be free from paying the heavy taxes which England had fixed upon them, and that they could go about their work in peace and quiet.

April brought warm, sunny days, and Anne no longer wore the knit hood and mittens, and had once more set her playhouse under the pine trees in order, and now Amanda with her doll often came to play with her.

"'Tis nearly a year ago since my father was captured by the British," said Anne one day as she and Amanda, followed by the white kitten, went out under the pine trees.

"Anne!" exclaimed Amanda, "I did not know what 'spy' and 'traitor' meant when I called those words at you."

Anne looked at her playmate smilingly. "You would not say them now, Amanda, would you?" she answered.

"Say them now!" repeated Amanda. "Why, Anne, you are my best friend, and your father a soldier. 'Twas but yesterday my father said that there was but one thing that Provincetown had to be proud of in this war, and that was John Nelson, your father, because he is the only soldier from the settlement."

Anne's cheeks flushed happily. "'Twas hard not to have my father," she said, "but he may come back any day now; Uncle Enos says so. And he is to live with us, and help Uncle Enos with the fishing. And then, Amanda, I shall be the happiest little girl in the settlement."

"To-morrow my mother is going to the marshes to gather young pine tips, and arrowroot, and young spruce tips and the roots of thoroughwort to brew beer with, said Amanda; "Amos and I are to go with her, and if your Aunt Martha be willing you can go with us. She plans to take something to eat and be away till past noon."

"I am sure I may go," replied Anne eagerly, "and we can bring home Mayflowers. There are many all along near the pine trees."

"Yes," said Amanda, "and will it not be fine to eat our dinner out-of-doors? Amos plans to start a fire and cook a fish for us, over it, this time, not under sand as he did when we were on the island."

Mrs. Stoddard gave her consent for Anne to go next day with the Carys. "I will bake you a molasses cake to carry," she said; "if it were a few weeks later you could call it a May party. In England, and I know it is now a custom in many of our towns, all the children gather and put flowers on their heads, and have a May-pole wreathed with flowers, and dance around it. And they choose a little girl for Queen of the May."

"Can we not do that, Aunt Martha, when May is really here?" asked Anne.

"Perhaps," replied Aunt Martha, "if the minister sees no objection, and if we get good news before that time, why, a May-day party would be a pretty thing. The boys could put up the May-pole near the spring, and there will be all sorts of wild things in blossom by that time."

When they started off for the marshes Anne told Amanda what her Aunt Martha had said, and Mrs. Cary and Amos were greatly interested. Amos said that he knew where he could get a fine pole, and Mrs. Cary said that the little girls could gather flowers and fasten them to the pole with vines and strings before it was set up.

"And there must be a big wreath fastened on top of the pole," said Mrs. Cary, "and by rights there should be long bright streamers coming down from the top for each to hold and twist in and out as they dance around it."

"Can we not take long strings and fasten flowers about them?" asked Anne.

"Why, yes, indeed!" replied Mrs. Cary. " 'Twill be better than any bright ribbons. Now we must surely have a May-day party. Near the spring will be the very place."

As they searched for thoroughwort, and picked the tender spruce and pine tips, they all talked of the coming May-day, but Amos soon began to look about for a good place to make his fire. He had brought the fish in a covered basket, and said that he knew he could cook it as well as if he had kettle to boil it in. He made a fire at a little distance from the woods, and then busied himself in putting up two crotched sticks, one on each side of the fire; a third stick rested across these two, and from it hung the fish, directly over the blaze.

Amos watched his fire very carefully, and kept a brisk blaze until the fish began to grow brown and steam. Then he declared that it was nearly cooked, and so let his fire die down until only a bed of smouldering coals remained.

They all thought the fish tasted as good as if it had been cooked in a pan or kettle, and Mrs. Cary had a fine cake of Indian meal, and with Anne's molasses cake they all said that it was the best dinner any one could have. The April sky was soft and blue, the sun warm, and Amos was sure that in a few days he could go in swimming.

"And it's only the nineteenth of April," said Anne.

Afterward these children always remembered the nineteenth of April, and would say, "That was the day we had our picnic at the marshes," and on that day the minutemen were gathered at Lexington and Earl Percy was urging his tired men to meet them, and the great battle which did so much to settle the fate of the Americans was fought.

But the people at Provincetown did not know of this until long afterward. If Anne had known on the day when she was so happy, thinking of the May-day to come, and watching Amos cook the fish over the fire, that her dear father with other brave men was at Cambridge on guard waiting for the British, who were determined to make a stand in their flight from the minutemen, and that on that very day her good friends, the Freemans, were hurrying away toward Watertown to escape the dangers of war which now centered about Boston, she would not have cared so much about the May-day plans.

"It would be well to ask all the grown people as well as the children to the May party," said Mrs. Cary, as the little party made its way toward home that afternoon. "I do not think there has ever been a May-day party before in the town, and it will be good for all of us to try and be cheerful."

Anne and Amanda looked at her wonderingly. The world seemed a very cheerful and happy place to both the little girls, and they could not know how anxious the older people were that the trouble with England might soon come to an end.

CHAPTER XVI

THE MAY PARTY

"A MAY-DAY party, eh?" said Elder Haven, when Anne and Amanda told him of the plan. "Why, I think it an excellent idea. It will surely be a pleasant sight to see the children dance about the May-pole, and I shall like well to come."

After Elder Haven had approved the parents could find nothing wrong in the idea, and all the children went Maying for arbutus and trailing evergreens to wind about the pole.

Early on the morning of May-day Amos and Jimmie were at the spring with a long smooth pole. The other children soon followed them, and Mrs. Starkweather came to show them how to fasten the wreath at the top and the long strings covered with vines and blossoms which Anne and Amanda, with the help of Mrs. Stoddard and the Starkweather boys, had made ready the day before.

"We used often to dance about a May-pole when I was a girl in Barnstable," said Mrs. Starkweather. "To be sure it is an old English custom, and just now England does not seem our friend, but 'tis a pleasant custom that we do well to folow. I know a little song that we all used to sing as we took hold of the bright streamers."

"I know that song," said Dannie; "you call it 'May Song.'"

"Why, yes," said Mrs. Starkweather, "I'm sure all my boys know it. I've sung them all to sleep by it; and 'tis one I sing about my work, for 'tis a cheerful and a merry lilt."

"It goes this way," said Dannie, and began to sing:

"Birds in the tree;
Humming of bees,
Wind singing over the sea;
Happy May-days,
Now do we praise,
As we dance gladly round the May tree."

As Dannie sang his mother and brothers joined in with him, and the other children listened in delight.

"Can you not sing it when we do 'dance round the May tree,' Aunt Starkweather?" asked Anne; "and if Dannie will sing it over to us a few times I am sure that we can all sing it, and then Elder Haven can hear us."

Dannie liked to sing, and he sang the little verse over and over again until all the children knew it, and until his mother said that they must all run home and make themselves tidy, and then come back, as the dance around the May-pole was to be at two o'clock.

"I do wish that Uncle Enos could see it," said Anne, as she put on her new white pinafore over her plaid dress, and fastened the coral beads around her neck; "I know well he would like to hear the song."

"The boats went out early and may get in in good time," said Aunt Martha.

"Mrs. Starkweather says that there is always a Queen of the May—a little girl whom the other children choose to wear a wreath on her head, and whatever the Queen tells them to do they must do all May-day," said Anne, as she and Mrs. Stoddard walked toward the spring, "but I do think the other children have forgotten all about it."

"What makes the children want to choose one to obey, I wonder," said Mrs. Stoddard, smiling down at Anne.

"It must be because 'tis a little girl whom they all like, and who is always kind and pleasant to the other children," said Anne. "If 'twas a King of the May we would all want Jimmie Starkweather; but there are not so many girls as boys."

The other children were all at the spring with bunches and wreaths of flowers, and Anne was surprised to see that a mound of sand had been heaped up and covered with pine boughs.

"What is that for?" she asked.

"That's a throne for the Queen," said Dannie Starkweather.

Mrs. Cary and Mrs. Starkweather were talking with the children, and as Anne came near they formed into a little circle round her, joining hands and singing:

> "Our May-queen,
>   Queen of the May,
>   We're ready to serve you
>   All this bright day."

Then Willie Starkweather, who was only four years old, took Anne's hand and led her to the "throne" and said, "You mutht thit down, Anne," for Willie lisped, "and I'll put the crown on."

So Anne sat down on the pine-covered sand-heap, and Willie put a wreath of fragrant arbutus on her head.

Captain Enos, hurrying up from the shore, thought it the prettiest sight he had ever seen. The tall pole, covered with green vines and bright blossoms, the children forming in a circle round Anne, and the pleasant May skies over all, seemed to the sailor to make a picture worth remembering.

Then came the dance round the May-pole and the song. By this time, the other men had come up from the shore; Elder Haven was there, and every one in the little settlement had gathered at the spring. It was a circle of happy faces, and when the time came for them all to start for their homes, each one said that Provincetown had never seen so pretty a sight.

" 'Tis something we shall like to think about," said Elder Haven to Jimmie Starkweather, as the two walked toward the Elder's house.

Anne was sure that it was the happiest day in her life. "I wish my father could have seen me, Aunt Martha," she said, as they walked toward home. " 'Twould please him well to know the children like me. 'Tis only a year since they did scorn me at the spring."

"You must forget about that, Anne," said Aunt Martha. "They chose you for Queen because you have been a pleasant child. You see, it matters not what they said before they knew you."

"Aunt Martha!" exclaimed Anne, suddenly looking up toward the harbor, "see! There are two big ships coming down the bay."

"We are not to be in peace long," said Mrs. Stoddard. "They are coming straight to anchorage."

Every one soon knew that the "Somerset" was back again, and now the English sailors took no trouble to be civil. They laid hands on provisions of all sorts, but nevertheless they brought good news.

William Trull found a chance to tell Captain Enos that the Americans had won the battle at Lexington. "We'll be in harbor here but a day or two," he added; "we must be back to watch the Americans at Charlestown." And, sure enough, the next morning the big ships had sailed away again, taking with them many things that the little settlement could ill spare.

As the summer days lengthened, Anne longed more and more for some news of her father. The battle of Bunker Hill had brought another triumph to the Americans, but the English vessels still cruised about the coast, making the fishermen careful about going far from shore.

"Uncle Enos, could we not go to Boston again and find my father?" Anne would ask, and Captain Enos would grow serious and shake his head, and say it would be too great a risk to undertake. So Anne helped Aunt Martha with the work of the house, played with her doll under the pine trees, and wandered about the shore with Amanda, but always thinking of her absent father, and wishing that she might go and find him.

"I am past nine years old. If I was a boy, I could sail a boat to Boston," she said to Amanda one day, as they went down to the beach to watch the fishing-boats come in.

"Yes," agreed Amanda; "I guess that Amos could sail a boat to Boston before he was nine."

"Then he could sail one there now," exclaimed Anne. "Oh, Amanda, wouldn't Amos sail us to Boston to find my father? Uncle Enos will not; he says 'tis not safe. But surely the English would not hurt two little girls and a boy. Would Amos be afraid?"

"Afraid of what?" Amos had come up beside them, and the sound of his voice made them jump.

"Afraid to sail a boat to Boston," explained Anne.

"That would be easy enough," declared the boy, "and I would like well to get the chance to sail father's 'Peggy' to Boston,"

"Will you, Amos? And take Amanda and me with you to find my father? I will take all the blame, indeed I will. And if we find him and bring him back, they will all think you a brave boy, Amos."

"They will not let us start," said Amos. "We'd have to put off in the night. But I'll do it. You girls must bring along something to eat, and we'll start at midnight."

"When?" asked Anne.

"To-night," answered the boy. "Why, 'twill be a greater adventure than any boy of this settlement ever had. If we make Boston, I may be made prisoner by the British," and Amos looked as happy over the prospect as Anne did at the thought of finding her father.

"Mistress Stoddard will not be pleased," cautioned Amanda.

"She did not greatly blame me before," said Anne. "She knows I want much to see my father, and Uncle Enos does not want to go. If we sail safely there and home, it will save Uncle Enos trouble. He will not have to go himself."

"Should we see Rose Freeman?" asked Amanda.

"It may be," said Anne.

"I would like well to go, if we could see her," Amanda said thoughtfully.

Amos was now full of plans for the trip. There would be a favoring tide at midnight, and he was sure they could sail out of the harbor and be well on their way by morning; and, giving the girls many cautions about being on the shore at the right time, he went happily off to look over the sloop "Peggy," and to wonder what Jimmie Starkweather would say if he knew that he, Amos, was going to sail a boat straight up to Boston!

CHAPTER XVII

THE SLOOP, "PEGGY"

THE sloop, "Peggy," was becalmed. Anne, Amanda and Amos looked over the smooth stretch of water, but there was not a ripple to be seen. Since sunrise, the boat had not moved. They had made the start at midnight, as they had planned, and had sailed away under a fair wind; but before the sun rose the wind had died away, and the mainsail now swung back and forth and the boat drifted slowly with the current.

None of the children had thought of bringing a jug of fresh water, and the salt fish and corn bread which they had brought along for food made them very thirsty.

"We're off Barnstable now," said Amos. "I've a mind to let the boat drift in nearer shore and anchor, and then row ashore in the tender and get some water."

"How far is Barnstable from Boston?" asked Anne.

"Miles and miles," answered Amos. "'Tis only about half-way up the cape from Provincetown."

THE BOAT BEGAN TO TIP

"Then we could not walk to Boston from there?"

"No," said Amos; "why should we walk? There'll be a good breeze come sunset. All we need is a good drink of water, and there's a water-jug in the cabin. I can take it ashore and fill it at some spring."

As the children talked, the current had carried the boat steadily toward shore, but now it did not move.

"She's stuck on a sand-bar," exclaimed Amos, "and the tide's turning. Perhaps I can walk ashore."

It was not long before the boat began to tip to one side, and as the tide went out, they found themselves on a sand-bar, a full half mile from shore. The water seemed to flow in little channels, like wide brooks, here and there, between the boat and the land, and Amos wondered if he could either jump or wade those channels. The hot July sun beat down upon them, they were very thirsty and uncomfortable, and Amanda began to wish herself at home.

"We ought not to have started," she said, ready to cry. "I know my mother won't like it, and Mistress Stoddard will not like it, either."

Anne was very quiet. She was thirsty, hot and uncomfortable, and being run aground on a sand-bar near a strange shore was a very different thing from her other prosperous voyage with Captain Enos. What if they should never reach Boston at all?

"They will all think that we have run away this time," said Amos, who had stepped over the side of the boat onto the sand-bar.

"Oh, no, they won't" said Anne. "I wrote on a smooth chip, 'Amanda and Amos and I have gone to Boston to find my father,' and put it on the kitchen table."

"I believe I could get across those channels some way," declared Amos, "and I am so thirsty that I'm going to try it."

Amanda brought him the small stone jug from the cabin, and telling the girls not even to step out of the boat until he came back, Amos started for the shore. They saw him wade the first channel, run across a long stretch of wet sand, cross the other channel and reach the shore safely.

"Goody!" exclaimed Amanda; "now he will find a spring, fill the jug and hurry back, and we can have a good drink of water," and she turned smilingly to Anne. But Anne was looking very sober. She had been thinking over her other trip, and now remembered what Mrs. Stoddard had said when she returned from Boston.

"Oh, Amanda!" she said, looking ready to cry, "when I ran off before with Uncle Enos, Aunt Martha did tell me that I must never do so again. Now I have disobeyed her, and perhaps she will not want me to live with her any more."

"Then you can live with your father," answered Amanda cheerfully.

"But my father was to live with us," said Anne. "He was to have the big, pleasant loft that looks toward the water, and was to help Uncle Enos with the fishing. Perhaps they will not want either of us since I have been so unruly and disobedient."

Amanda longed to tell Anne that she should have a home with her, but she remembered that the white kitten had to be given away because they could not afford to keeep it, and so kept silent.

"I hope Amos will not linger," she said, after a little silence. "He forgets that we are as thirsty as he is."

The little girls watched the shore anxiously, expecting every minute to see Amos hurrying back with a jug full of fresh water, but time passed and he did not come.

"I think the tide has turned," said Amanda. "See, the channels are widening every minute, If Amos does not come soon the water will be too deep. Oh, dear! I am afraid something has befallen him."

"What could befall him?" questioned Anne. " 'Tis a smooth and pleasant shore, with much taller trees than grow about Provincetown. He is just playing about and has forgotten us."

Anne was nearly right, for after Amos had found a fine boiling spring and had drunk all he wanted and then filled his jug, he had sat down to rest under a wide-spreading oak tree. The day was hot, he was very tired and sleepy, having been awake all the night before, and without forgetting the "Peggy" or her crew, he dropped gently off to sleep. The tide came in, lifted the "Peggy" from the sand-bar and a gentle breeze carried her steadily out from shore, and Amos slept on, knowing nothing of what had happened. The sun was very low in the western sky when he awoke. He sat up, rubbed his eyes, snatched up the jug and ran to the shore, but there was no boat to be seen.

Amos was now thoroughly frightened. He ran up and down the quiet shore, calling the name of his boat and shouting, "Amanda!" "Anne!" at the top of his voice. The shadows of the summer night deepened, a little haze rose over the water, and Amos, crouching down near the water's edge, waited for night to come.

"I now I shall never sleep any more," he whispered to himself, hardly daring to think of what might happen to the little girls. He wished that he had lowered the mainsail before coming ashore.

"I ought to have dropped anchor, anyway," he said aloud, and almost forgot to be hungry in his anxiety.

The shadows grew deeper, night settled down on land and sea and Amos went fast asleep again, with his bare feet almost within reach of the waves that rolled so softly up over the smooth sand.

Anne and Amanda watched the tide come in about the "Peggy," and soon felt the boat move under them. Then the mainsail filled and swung out, as the breeze came up.

"Try and steer ashore, Amanda," exclaimed Anne.

"I dare not touch the rudder," said Amanda. "Whenever I have been in a boat, my father has told me to sit still; and I do think it is the best thing we can do now, Anne."

"Mayhap the wind will take us home again," said Anne, "and then your father will come back and find Amos."

"More like 'twill take us straight out to sea," said Amanda.

" 'Tis all my fault," said Anne; "I did prevail on you and Amos to come."

"We both liked well to come," answered Amanda stoutly. "Amos should have known better, for he is older. But he likes a risk over well, and now he can play shipwrecked to his heart's desire."

"My eyes are heavy with sleep," said Anne. "Let us say the small prayer that Elder Haven taught us and sleep a little. 'Tis dark and foggy; we can see nothing."

Amanda reached out her sunburned little hand and clasped Anne's, and they repeated aloud the prayer, asking for help and protection, which Elder Haven had taught them; then, curling themselves up in the bottom of the boat, they went fast asleep.

But the "Peggy" did not sail far. The wind died away, and the boat drifted with the tide. When the little girls awoke it was bright sunshine, and a big ship was coming slowly down upon them.

" 'Tis a Britisher!" Amanda exclaimed; "like as not she's bound for England and will carry us straight off," and Amanda began crying bitterly.

Before Anne could answer there came a hail from the ship, and Anne and Amanda called back, "Sloop 'Peggy'! Sloop 'Peggy'!" as loudly as they could, as they had heard Provincetown captains do in answer to hails from harbor boats.

It was not long before the big vessel was near enough for the sailors to distinguish that there were only two little girls on board the drifting sloop and a man was ready with a stout boat-hook, which he grappled about the "Peggy's" mast, and a big man with reddish hair and blue eyes slid down a rope and swung himself on board the sloop.

"Zounds!" exclaimed the sailor, "if 'tis not the little Provincetown maid again! And adrift like this. I'll have to take you to England and let Betsey and Hannah take care of you!"

Before he had finished both Anne and Amanda had begun to cry. They were sure now that they should never see home again, and William Trull had some trouble in convincing them that he did not mean to take them to Engand.

But the captain had small patience with the delay, and called out that 'twas best to sink the sloop rather than lose a fair wind out of harbor.

"I cannot be leaving two helpless maids adrift," William Trull called back. "They are from the Provincetown settlement."

"Take them back to it, if you like, and find your way across the Atlantic as best you may," retorted the English captain angrily. "We can't stand by for such folly."

Poor William Trull looked at the little girls in dismay. To be left stranded on American territory was the last thing he desired.

"Can't you tow our boat down to Provincetown?" pleaded Anne. "We won't hurt you."

"Ha! ha!" laughed the captain, and even William Trull joined in the laughter of the crew, while Anne and Amanda wondered why the sailors laughed. "Well," and the captain's voice was more friendly as he leaned over his ship's railing and gazed down at the little girls, "if you won't run us down we'll take you along that far. You can stay on the sloop, Trull, till we get near the tip of the cape. 'Tis plain American children are not easily frightened."

The sloop was now taken in tow, and although the little girls pleaded that a boat be sent to find Amos, William Trull shook his head.

" 'Twill not do," he declared, "to ask it of the captain; and if the boy be a smart boy he'll make his way home, never fear."

It was some comfort to Amanda to declare that Amos was the smartest boy in the settlement; that he could make fire as Indians did, and that he knew many ways of snaring birds and fish.

"Never fear for a boy like that," said the sailor.

Anne was eager to ask him if he knew anything of her father, and William Trull owned that he did.

" 'Twas your father who some way got word to Newburyport and Portsmouth men to be ready to fight," he said. " 'Twas cleverly done, they tell me, but no one has found out how."

"I know," said Anne, "because I helped." Then remembering Captain Stoddard's caution, she put her hand over her mouth. "I must not tell," she said.

The sailor looked at her in astonishment. "Even the children are 'rebels,' " he declared, "and helping when chance comes. 'Tis a great country. I'll not question you, child, but I'll tell my little girls about you, and that you helped to send the English home. Your own father will soon be telling you how the Americans drove the English; but you must keep a kind thought for me."

"Oh, I do wish you would stay and be an American, Mr. William Trull, and bring your little girls to live in Provincetown," said Anne.

"Who knows?" said the sailor. "It may be I'll be coming back with my family. I like this country well. Your father will be coming to Provincetown soon, never fear," he added, "for now Boston port is open to all, and the fishermen are going in and out as they please."

Amanda had not been much interested in what the sailor had to say. She was thinking that Amos must be very hungry; and when William Trull climbed aboard the big vessel and the sloop dropped behind near the Provincetown shore, she was greatly rejoiced.

It was not long that the "Peggy" was alone. Men on shore had been watching and were quick to recognize the sloop, and a boat was sent out. Amanda recognized that her father was in it, as well as Captain Enos and Jimmie Starkweather, and called out in delight. There was an anxious crowd on the beach, and Mrs. Stoddard and Amanda's mother ran eagerly forward to greet the little girls, and to ask what had become of Amos.

It was soon evident that Jimmie Starkweather and the other boys were inclined to be envious of Amos's good furtune; and when Mr. Cary made his own boat ready to sail for Barnstable to bring Amos home Jimmie was very proud to be selected to accompany him.

"How shall we ever feel safe about thee, child?" said Mrs. Stoddard, as she and Anne walked toward home. "Are you always to be seeking your father without telling us? If you had but waited you would have saved us all this worry, and Amos would now be safe at home."

"But I have news, Aunt Martha," pleaded Anne. "Mr. William Trull told me my father might soon be with us. I will not leave you again, unless, indeed, you no longer want me."

"Of course we want you, Anne. But I have better news than the English sailor gave you. Look! Here comes some one whom you will be glad to see," but before she had finished speaking Anne had sprung forward with an exclamation of delight, for her father was coming down the path to the shore.

"I came down in one of Mr. Freeman's fishing-boats," he explained, as, hand in hand, he and Anne walked back to join Mrs. Stoddard. Anne danced along happily, and Mrs. Stoddard smiled as she looked at the little girl.

"And now I hope for peace," declared the good woman. "Anne will not let you go again, John Nelson. You will have to be content to stay in Provincetown."

The next day Elder Haven came to see John Nelson to hear more about the great triumphs of the Americans; and when Anne's father told him of Captain Stoddard's trip to Newburyport, with Anne carrying the important message for the Newburyport patriots, the good clergyman held up his hands in wonder. "She is a brave little maid," he said. "It should be put on record that a maid of Provincetown helped the Americans to win their just cause against King George. Indeed it should."

"She is a brave child," agreed Captain Enos. "I was sure of it when I heard her defend her father at the spring," and the good captain chuckled at the remembrance of Anne's battle with the Cary children, who were now her staunchest friends.

"Amos is safe home, and proud enough; he is lording it well over his mates," said Elder Haven. "You must not run away again, Anne," he added more gravely, resting a gentle hand on the dark head.

"No, oh, no!" replied Anne, "not unless my father and Aunt Martha and Uncle Enos go with me."

CPSIA information can be obtained
at www.ICGtesting.com
Printed in the USA
BVHW03s2151050718
520948BV00001B/5/P

9 781557 093318